Praise for
A Million Skies

"In telling the story of her harrowing journey through bipolar disorder without sugar-coating the darkest, grittiest chapters, Abigail Alleman gives permission to all who have been silenced by shame and fear to name and claim our own chapters of brokenness, trauma, and loss. Few writers bring the kind of courage, honesty, and vulnerability to the page that Alleman generously offers us in every paragraph. In a culture that continues to stigmatize mental illness, she has overcome her own fear, shame, and doubt, persevering to give hope and encouragement to others who are floundering in darkness. I am profoundly grateful to Alleman for her bravery, for her authenticity, and, above all, for so selflessly giving us the gift of herself and her unvarnished story. In doing so, she has gifted us with a powerful testimony of God's truth, hope, goodness, and love."

—**Michelle DeRusha,** author of *True You*

"I don't think this book was meant to be read in one sitting, but that's how it happened for me. I was blown away. This story of one woman's triumphant victory simply wouldn't let me go. Maybe we all need to know that victory is possible, no matter what we are facing. Maybe we all need to know that the voices whispering defeat in our ears can't drown out the voice of truth that we were made to hear. *A Million Skies* is more than a book. It's a victory march that will point you to the healing you've always hoped was possible."

—**Jennifer Dukes Lee,** author of *Growing Slow* and *It's All Under Control*

"*A Million Skies* artfully highlights the ways that beauty and brokenness coexist in our story. Abigail Alleman shows us that 'we're more than the bleak skies of our low points,' but God is also with us in those dark moments. This is a helpful book to normalize conversations around mental health, especially in the church."

—**Michelle Ami Reyes,** Vice President, Asian American Christian Collaborative; author, *Becoming All Things*

"Beautifully written and emotionally raw, *A Million Skies* invites readers to connect intimately with oneself, God, and others on their mental health journeys. In honest moments of living with the mania and depression of bipolar disorder as well as the terrors of mental wards and hallucinations, Abigail Alleman allows us to witness her move out of fear, shame, and isolation into a life of courage, hope, and deep connection to Jesus. Readers will find Alleman a trusted companion and guide if they live with bipolar disorder or if they desire to better understand anyone living with this diagnosis."

—**Heather Holleman,** PhD, speaker, author of *Seated with Christ* and *Guarded by Christ*

"In *A Million Skies*, Abigail Alleman gently takes us by the hand and leads us through a story familiar to any who've walked through a life-altering hardship. Abigail's beautifully written story brings peace to the heart, hope to the soul, and silences shame surrounding the ways we all struggle."

—**Heather Creekmore,** podcast host, author of *The Burden of Better* and *Compared to Who?*

"*A Million Skies* is an amazing example of how the gospel removes the masks we hide behind. God's faithfulness is put on display as Abigail Alleman moves gracefully and powerfully through her story of mental illness, giving hope to all who've struggled, and understanding for all who haven't. Alleman takes us on a thrilling journey that is unforgettable and deeply relatable as she shows the complexity of living with bipolar disorder while being focused on living for the glory of God."

—**Jon Adams,** Discipleship Pastor at Orlando Baptist Church

"In *A Million Skies*, Abigail Alleman does a fantastic job of being transparent, as we all should, so that those suffering don't have to suffer alone. Her words are beautiful brushstrokes of insight, hope, and truth. In this book are pathways out of the darkness and into the light."

—**Dr. Rex A. Birkmire,** MD and Psychiatrist

"Anyone who has walked the dark valley after having been diagnosed with a mental health issue knows the pain, shame, stigma, and deep longing that often ensues. They long to know, 'Is there hope for me?' Abigail Alleman shares openly and vulnerably of her journey through the wilderness of bipolar disorder to offer others hope. That experience was her conduit through which she came to know her own need and know God in a deeper and more personal way. She reminds the reader that despite the label of their struggle (bipolar disorder, depression, anxiety, single, divorced, etc.), they are still created in God's image, beautiful and whole."

—**Dr. Michelle L. Bengtson,** award-winning author of *Hope Prevails* and *Breaking Anxiety's Grip*

"Mental illness, anguish, grief, loss, shame. If this is your reality, even just a hint of your life, this book will be a gift to you! Abigail Alleman takes us into the depths of her journey in darkness, the unveiling of her idols, the destruction of her dreams. 'How would I ever become someone more than a woman covered in the questionable fog of an unstable mind?' she asked. Gratefully she doesn't leave us there. She artfully, humbly, beautifully leads us to hope and victory."

—**Judy Douglass,** author of *When You Love a Prodigal*, speaker, encourager, Director, Cru Women's Resources

"Abigail Alleman's transparency in her journey is something that has been desperately needed, especially in the Evangelical community. In this 'instant society' with instant solutions, we have to recognize that this is a journey that for most of us will include 'the dark night of the soul.' But if we embrace that night fully, as Abigail has shown us, on the other side we have new dimensions of strength, courage, and understanding of the God who loves us with an everlasting love."

—**David Martin,** lifelong pastor, counselor, and hospital chaplain

"It's rare to witness such an offering of love and courage as Abigail delivers in this moving memoir. Her compassion for readers—especially those who have experienced mental illness—is stunning. She encourages them in their faith while prompting them to recognize mental illness for what it is and learn to care for themselves, body, mind, and soul. If the church could hear more searingly honest voices like Abigail's, then millions of Christians suffering in silence might begin to step forward and share their stories with the rest of us, allowing us to know, love, and support them where they are."

—**Carrie Morris,** Licensed Marriage & Family Therapist, Wedgewood Circle Artist, and Member of Redbud Writers Guild

"In *A Million Skies,* Abigail Alleman shares a profound and hauntingly honest look at the pain, shame, and lies of mental illness. Hers is a story of ravaging mental illness and the toll it took on her reputation, family, and ministry. But to stop there would be to miss how God met her in the wilderness. Chapter by chapter, Abigail shows how she moved from despair to hope, from shame to freedom, from suffering to redemption. Abigail bravely and candidly shares her pain, giving others permission to acknowledge theirs, and offers practical and biblical hope to live well with an ongoing mental diagnosis. This book provides authentic, scriptural support for those living with mental illness, for those who love someone with mental illness, and for the body of Christ as we live alongside those with mental illness."

—**Lisa Appelo,** author *Life Can Be Good Again*

SECURE IN
GOD'S STRENGTH
WHEN YOUR MIND
CAN'T REST

A MILLION SKIES

ABIGAIL ALLEMAN

LEAFWOOD
PUBLISHERS
an imprint of Abilene Christian University Press

A MILLION SKIES
Secure in God's Strength When Your Mind Can't Rest

LEAFWOOD
P U B L I S H E R S
an imprint of Abilene Christian University Press

Copyright © 2022 by Abigail Alleman

ISBN 978-1-68426-400-1 | LCCN 2021036927

Printed in the United States of America

Published in association with The Gates Group, 1403 Walnut Lane, Louisville, KY 40223.

LIBRARY OF CONGRESS CATALOGING-IN-PUBLICATION DATA
Names: Alleman, Abigail, 1974- author.
Title: A million skies : secure in God's strength when your mind can't rest / Abigail Alleman.
Description: Abilene, Texas : Leafwood Publishers, [2022] | Includes bibliographical references.
Identifiers: LCCN 2021036927 | ISBN 9781684264001 (paperback) | ISBN 9781684269365 (epub)
Subjects: LCSH: Manic-depressive persons—Biography. | Manic-depressive illness—Popular works. | Manic-depressive illness—Religious aspects—Christianity. | Depressed persons—Biography. | Depression, Mental—Popular works. | Depression, Mental—Religious aspects—Christianity.
Classification: LCC RC516 .A378 2022 | DDC 616.89/50092 [B]—dc23/eng/20211001
LC record available at https://lccn.loc.gov/2021036927

Cover design by ThinkPen Design, LLC | Interior text design by Sandy Armstrong, Strong Design

Leafwood Publishers is an imprint of Abilene Christian University Press
ACU Box 29138 | Abilene, Texas 79699

1-877-816-4455 | www.leafwoodpublishers.com

22 23 24 25 26 27 28 / 7 6 5 4 3 2 1

CONTENTS

To Jared,
You have been my rock,
my encourager,
my beloved companion,
and
truest friend
on this long road home.

And
to my earthly
Abba Daddy,
You prayed me through every storm,
until you found your eternal rest.
I will miss you
until I am home
in those Heavenly Abba
arms with you.

READY FOR A NEW DAY

There are a million ways to see our lives, and those views can shift like the skies above us.

On clear, bright, sunny days, when there is a perfect balance of warmth and coolness, everything tastes sweeter, and the crisp air exhilarates us. We would all love to spend every day under those kinds of skies.

But the reality of our broken world also means that we sometimes dwell under dark, frigid skies on nights when no stars or moons illuminate our path. We find ourselves in the pitch black with stark fear as our companion.

Even when the sun is shining, looming clouds may threaten to overtake us with whipping winds and vicious storms. We can become as frightened little children while worrying about a potential storm.

Lurking just on the edges of our vision are the threats of the unthinkable. Hurricanes that can flatten our homes and uproot our support systems. Tornados that can suddenly appear on the horizon and kill in a heartbeat. So many threats, whether real or imagined, pelt our hearts like giant hailstones and leave us battered and bruised.

Mental illness has clouded my life's journey, often overwhelming me with the shifting, perilous realities of bipolar disorder. At times, I have not known what the next second will bring, but I have been certain that death was waiting nearby. It can be nearly impossible to find the anchor of the sun or the steadiness of a healing rain when in the middle of a tumultuous and ever-changing gale.

Yet as I continued battling my elements, the views of my life have been radically altered. Not every day is bright and sunny, but today I regularly dwell under blue skies. A lot of hard work, consistent treatment, and great faith helped me navigate a course toward a triumphant vista. I know my victory is real, and I know others can follow a similar path to sunlit horizons.

It is my deep and sincere desire that anyone grappling with mental illness will know they are not alone in this struggle. Sadly, mental illness so often feels lonely, cold, and bleak. But, friend, we are in this together. I promise, if you stay in the process, you will see real change.

In the pages that follow, I share stories of my struggle honestly, vulnerably, and with great self-compassion. I bring you my story because I want to offer hope for yours. It's a gritty road at times, but I believe we can and will find our way together to a stunningly hued sunrise. Maybe we will just catch glimpses of the dawn at first, but if we remain on the journey, our moments of hope will lengthen and deepen.

So get ready. Put off whatever prevents you from believing that the warm sun can break through your storm and that your future can be bright and calm. An azure sky and the saturated cascade of a brilliant rainbow can be yours.

A new day is needed for all who struggle with mental illness. It is time to get rid of the stigma, the shame, the fear. It is time to let beauty, freedom, and love rule in our lives.

As we prepare for this new day, I do not mean to say that our skies will never grow dark again. As long as we live in a fallen world, there will be struggles. But the hope of clearer, refreshing tomorrows can help us experience victory even in places of defeat and deep discouragement.

You may have picked up this book as a gift for a friend on a mental illness journey and are wondering if there is anything you might glean from these pages. I believe there is. Mental illness is not the only threat to life's clear skies. The storm clouds in your life may arise from chronic pain, physical ailments, a broken relationship, debilitating grief, or deep disappointment. Whatever burden you carry in your life, I believe the truths I share in this book can help you find a place of rest, too.

A Million Skies is intended to be a song from God to your heart. In these pages, I have written my story. But my story is also God's story of how he can bring you from death to life. This happens once and forever through belief in Jesus Christ but also in every moment, as the Spirit of Christ makes all things new. New in you and then through you, into this world and its every sky.

Don't stop reading because you doubt you will ever find the strength to see clearer skies. If you experience one bright day in a hundred darker ones, this journey will be worth the effort.

We can take heart because our savior has faced every sky-shadowing storm and vanquished them with his light, which cannot be overcome. Jesus promises he is the light in every sky, and he proved the reality of that promise by overcoming the total darkness of death. With him, all things are possible.

May we claim the reality of that promise. Intimately. Deeply. Hand in hand with one another and empowered by the God of all goodness and beauty dwelling among us, we will boldly walk into a new day.

1

MENTAL ILLNESS DOESN'T WRITE MY STORY
From Weakness to Strength

November 2015

I shifted nervously on the caramel-colored couch in my therapist's office. The Florida sunshine fell as a gentle waterfall that autumn day. But I wasn't shining. I was battling burdens of guilt, shame, and fear while trying to come to grips with my bipolar disorder.

I had been diagnosed only a few months earlier, in the wake of devastation and trauma. The identification of my mental illness had removed a boulder from my chest, giving me something concrete to explain what I had been experiencing for fifteen years. Yet, as can easily happen with a mental illness, I began allowing myself to be defined by my diagnosis.

This label didn't reveal itself as neon letters scrawled across my life. Instead, it subtly weaved insidious roots into the core of my being, making me feel as though each day held shadow, something lurking that was bigger than life. I feared a pending storm would either wreak full-blown destruction or ratchet up my anxiety as the tempest skirted around me.

On this particular morning of mundane—all drama held at bay—I folded my notes from the session and put them in my purse. As I prepared to leave, my therapist said, "I want you to begin to see your bipolar disorder as a blessing, a strength."

I paused and blinked. She might as well have told me to hang the stars. It was an impossible thing, what she was asking. How would I even begin?

Mood disorders like bipolar trap people on a roller coaster of emotions, plunging them from dizzying highs to bottomless lows. Each person's experience is slightly different, but I think many can relate when I describe my own experiences.

I have been through seasons of "hypomania" filled with an exhilarating explosion of ideas and creative processes. However, this intense mental stimulation cannot be sustained, and is eventually followed by sleeplessness. This lack of sleep, coupled with a continual cycling of thoughts, lead me to delusional thinking, spiritual visions, and hallucinations. I've been hospitalized twice in this state because I lost touch with reality and the world around me.

The proverbial truth that what goes up must come down is demonstrated in mood swings that produce volatility and irrationality among other behaviors. When my mania abates, I then feel the weight of depression. As I am writing this book, I have more than twenty years of experience with bipolar disorder. I have spent about 95 percent of my unstable times in depression and 5 percent in bouts of mania. However, that 5 percent of time has produced the most devastating experiences. With my strong tendency toward depression, trying to stabilize after a manic episode felt like trying to stand upright while shouldering two-ton weights.

In light of this knowledge, I drove home pondering my therapist's words. How could my erratic behavior, which hurt those I loved most, be viewed as a blessing? How could the same chemical imbalance that landed me in a foreign hospital for two weeks be seen as a strength? In so many ways, I had absolutely no idea.

Unnaming Reflection

Yet, looking deeper into my recent journey with mental illness, I inched toward my therapist's words. I realized I had seen myself at my worst in the last year and I had survived this intense time with my sanity intact. Therefore, there *was* a strength to be found beyond all the mess, and maybe there was a way to see my journey with bipolar disorder positively. For all the pain and struggle, I had come through stronger, more resilient. It was easy to fear that mental illness would defeat me once and for all. So, in a paradoxical way, I was grateful for the experience of bipolar disorder because it made an understanding of inward strength possible.

I felt a touch of open space, the grace to crack the door to this new perspective, this sky of promise. I thought that if I could capture one moment—one layer of warm brightness—at a time, I could illuminate the darkness. But I didn't know how to make that goal a reality.

I could still see clearly the whole picture of my tumultuous journey, the traumatic events of my hospital stay, and the weeks leading up to it. As a person who believes in the spiritual realm, I see a connection between the lies we believe and the nature of an illness like bipolar disorder. When stable, I believe I can hear the voice of God and his truth. When in a state of mania or depression, my judgment is off, and it is easy to believe lies, which are generated by the evil one. In my worst days, these lies took up residence, and they undid me.

Dan B. Allender refers to this evil as "unnaming." He writes, "In those moments of unnaming, when we have lost ourselves, we must remember to return to our past redemptions to find God's marks of glory on our abandonment, betrayal and shame."[1] In the episodes in my recent past, an unnaming process had occurred. The essentials of true identity were lost. My diagnosis and its milieu took the precious gift of *Abigail*, Hebrew for *source of joy*, and all the meaning that my name entailed. Bipolar was a dark lens defining and confining me.

That dark state was not what my loved ones wanted for me and definitely not what an intimate, personal, naming God desired for me. Even when I was soul-weary, truth declared there was something more. I needed to make a fundamental change in how I viewed my life. And right now was the time to do it.

In the days, months, and years after the therapist startled me with her words, I sifted through my memories and reflected on my past. And I came to see clearly that my life had been saved repeatedly. In fact, the redemptions have been too many to count.

Of course, God had placed ongoing gifts in my life:

- A twin sister to walk alongside me through our family's difficult circumstances and the parts of me triggered by those circumstances.
- The faith of generations passed down by grandmothers who crocheted blankets and handmade lace doilies with beautiful intricacy.
- The ever-present bowed head of my daddy as he stormed the gates of heaven.

- The delicious delight of my mom's homemade savory and sweet creations, made with worn hands and a heart full of love.

All these gifts spoke of an intentional care that was so tender and freely given. Graces like these rained down like falling stars to collect.

And there were more dramatic events. My sharp-witted, cool-under-pressure mother had saved me from choking to death when I was four years old. And I survived without a scratch on me or my car when I spun out in heavy traffic on Interstate 95 near Boston, doing a cycle of 360s. When I was safe at home, I had called my mother and wept. I had survived at ages four and at twenty-four. Surely, I concluded, God meant for me to be alive.

And just a few months before my pivotal therapist appointment, I had nearly died, most likely due to an allergic reaction to a heavy dose of sedative, a story that I tell in more detail in Chapter Two. During my near-death days in a hospital in Budapest, Hungary, a thousand and more voices had been lifted in prayer for me. There, too, God was speaking life. At least these three times, I had balanced on death's edge—yet, I lived. During my recovery from the trauma in Hungary, I could almost hear the Spirit whisper, "I don't want you to just survive your life—I want you to thrive in it."

I again felt that Spirit-sentiment palpably as I grappled with the radical words of my therapist: "I want you to begin to see your bipolar disorder as a blessing, a strength." As I began to embrace God's desire for me to truly live, I was starting to unfurl in those shame-ridden places, opening to the faintest pinprick of a brightening sky. By no means was I going to stop any time soon.

Beautifully Made

A couple weeks after that mind-shifting appointment with my therapist, I was walking on the sidewalk outside our apartment. It wasn't the place I would expect to receive a grand revelation, but it is the place I received one while listening to an audiobook by Timothy Keller about prayer.

At one point, Keller explained that no one person could have written the Bible, with its various emotions, intellectual connections, and manifestations of wisdom.[2] The implication of what he was saying stunned me, and I could feel a dawning enlightenment of how I should view myself. While I certainly could not have written all of the Bible, the ways I'm wired make it easier for me to understand certain parts. For example, in the Psalms, I connect with both the heights of praise and the depths of crying out. This isn't incidental, given the cycles of highs and lows fostered by my bipolar disorder. Also, the left, analytical side of my brain connects with the books of the law and the right side of my brain treasures the artistry of the prophetic books. In this moment, I started to see that when I was stable and treated, the heights and depths of my emotions and my ways of thinking could shine like the assets they were.

As I was listening to Keller, the Holy Spirit began helping me understand how I was made and how I could reclaim my past. I had been beautifully made, and I began to take ownership of my story. I began to recognize that when a great, chilling darkness hovered over my memory, hissing ugly words like *relapse*, *breakdown*, and *insanity*, the evil one was conspiring to hold me hostage. But now I was hearing a new voice, and a battle cry started welling up within me: "No more!"

My friend, when we stare down evil, we must declare, "You will not have me!" Our next step must be to trust in the goodness of our Creator, to see how we have been made and recognize that we are made for so much more.

Taking on an Active Role

When I worked at a camp for children who had special needs, I learned the "hand over hand" method for helping kids cut, color, eat, and do just about anything else. I would place my hand over theirs, assisting them to make a craft or get nutrients into their precious bodies. I have used the same technique with my own children, feeling their darling, chubby hands underneath mine as they learned how to write their name, draw a person, shoot a basketball, play tennis, and more.

And so it is with us and God. He's hand over hand in all the minutiae of our lives, showing us how to make the next move, pen the next mark on the paper, hit the ball, pick up the phone. He is authoring my story and yours, and he calls forth our deepest selves to write with him. Sometimes as we grow in exquisite ways, it's difficult to distinguish between hands because our movements have become fused with his.

The strength I gain from my bipolar disorder—I know now—is that my struggle allows me to see my past and present more fully, more victoriously. Granted, my struggle sometimes takes me into a dark abyss, but I believe that God can and does redeem the pain, even the torture that I've endured. And I have faith that he will offer that redemption again and again.

While we might think we would be better off escaping what has happened in the past, I agree with Allender when he says, "Without our past we are hollow and plastic beings who have only common names and conventional stories. When we enter into our story at the point we lost our name, we are most likely to hear the whisper of our new name. Remember, God is still writing."[3]

We're more than the bleak skies of our low points. We're more than the torment of our mental storms. We're more than forecasts of gray skies like those I experienced in the long, damp winters in Hungary. From deep within me rises a force of will that calls me to be fully alive to the clear, crisp, glorious nature of longed-for days. I'm choosing life over death, promise over destruction, love over hate—an azure sky over the black of night.

I want to inspire you to take a white-knuckled hold on the redemption of your story. Open the eyes of your heart to see what has been "bought back" or redeemed. This has become the linchpin by which my entire world of thinking and seeing holds together. Jesus and his redemption.

Always Present

The true light, Jesus the Word who took on flesh, came and faced all the horrors and alienation of our world (John 1:14). He faced the all-out temptation of Satan at the peak of his weakness and hunger from forty days without food and drink (Matt. 4:1–11). He breathed the healing life into the sick and weak. At the cross, he faced the darkest sky ever known, when his intimate, always-existing relationship with his Father was completely severed. Yet he overcame.

His story is the one that ultimately owns my story and yours too. His resurrection life, defeating death and the grave, speaks acutely into my journey with mental illness. Jesus must be the focus of my eyes, the perception of my skies, no matter what they hold or how deep their darkness. Because of who he is and his guarantee that I've been made in his image, my created light has found his, piercing every layer of gray and black.

The belief that God could and would redeem the rampant brokenness of my life has fundamentally changed me. I have leaned hard into the promise and called forth a more-precious-than-gold and steelier resolve to cry out with Job: "I know that my redeemer lives, and that in the end he will stand on the earth. And after my skin has been destroyed, yet in my flesh I will see God; I myself will see him with my own eyes" (Job 19:25–27).

Whose words on grief, life destruction, and redemption could stand taller than Job's? Although none of his issues described in the Bible include diagnosed mental illness, Job nearly lost his mind because of the pain he endured. Yet in the thick of his emotional turmoil, he clung to and cried out with those words of enduring faith.

My friend, I know you are hurting, but you aren't meant to linger in a dark, damp corner, folded up in pain and feeling utterly alone. You're meant to bask in the sunshine and its healing warmth. You are made for something more than suffering. Your struggles were not—and are not—against flesh and blood. Instead, they are against the powers of darkness that want to take you down. My friend, the evil one is planning to wreck and destroy your life. But God is present. Look to the skies and don't be afraid of the storm.

As my therapist challenged me, so I challenge you. Think of your mental illness, your hardship, as a strength. It does not need to define you or limit you. Your story is still being written, and good is present. Are you able to believe that something greater is waiting for you if you stay the course and refuse to lose heart?

2

LEARNING HOW TO SEE
From Despair to Hope

February 2015

Light funneled through the thick-paned window of *Szent Imre Kórház* (St. Henry's Hospital), winding its way over various machines and hospital beds before rising to touch my eyelids. I awoke. After three days of sedatives and mental mayhem, I clearly and brightly came alive to a new day.

Kati, a doctor who loved Jesus, sat beside my bed, hands folded. When she saw me open my eyes, she said, "I am so happy you are awake. I have been praying for you." With that simple sentence, the Holy Spirit greeted me with one of the more than thousand voices that had been praying for my life.

As myriad tubes were removed from my body, I felt the presence of God. It was no accident that I was alive. I had been unable to breathe when I was rushed to the ICU. I could remember only a couple of moments from the last three days, but I knew I had almost died. This truth was clear—I was intended for life and to life I had come.

I wasn't yet ready to label as "hope" my emotions in these waking moments. I was mentally still somewhat engaged in my inward vision of angels and demons, spiritually charged, cataclysmic scenes, which had captured me in the past weeks of insomnia. But I knew this light, this grandeur, bore promise. Something true was ahead of me.

My beloved husband, Jared, came to visit me later that evening, his face alight with joy and relief. My mentor, Barb, also came. It was clear worry had consumed them, but now they believed I would be okay although they recognized the long road ahead.

When things are reduced to life and death, little else matters except breathing. In and out, my breath rose and fell like music to my loved ones.

The weeks prior to this awakening had been shrouded in stormy skies and the sheer void of darkness—the environment of evil itself. Nevertheless, morning had come—simple, persistent, life-giving sunlight that penetrated the darkness. It spoke of victory.

Part of an Epic Story

That Sunday morning felt to me like the moment of sunrise when the wizard Gandalf arrived at the battle of Helm's Deep, just as he had predicted. "Look to my coming on the first light of the fifth day, at dawn look to the east," Gandalf said in *Lord of the Rings: The Two Towers*, the epic movie based on the novel by J. R. R Tolkien. Gandalf comes in gleaming garb, riding on a dazzling white horse with the Rohirrim cavalry. Soon they descend upon the troops of Saruman, and what was a bleak battle full of darkness transforms into great victory for Middle Earth.[1]

Am I saying my life is epic? I think it is. And so is yours. We are each meant for a new day. One in which there will be no feeling of "less than," one that will be perfect in grace and beautiful in wholeness. One day we will live in a forever day that cannot be marred. But until then, our lives display the gleaming reality of our living, reigning redeemer, who is more brilliant than the noonday sun.

As I returned to life in that hospital room, I glimpsed the warming light of a certain hope. The light offered a symbol of triumphant faith and a promise that sleepless nights of despair and manic days of horrific visions would not continue ceaselessly.

Before I awoke that Sunday morning, I could hardly believe this mania could ever end. My mind had been unstable, and I had lost touch with reality in the weeks before I had been admitted to the hospital. My erratic behavior was at its height when they placed me here, and I felt so out of control. But I was certain that the hospital was an evil place and that people there intended to harm me. I believed only that the voices I was hearing were true.

In this state, I came under the effect of the sedatives I was given. I had not flat-lined or been declared dead. Nonetheless, nothing was left of me in those dark days. The voices I trusted led me to try to leave the hospital through the window. I didn't intend to jump, just to raise my hands beyond the iron bars so God Three-in-One could lift me to heaven. I was done with the horror I experienced in those days. I was done with my shredded mind seeing and hearing lies of great doom. I was done with the claws of doubt ripping into my faith.

After my second attempt to escape through the window, they molded my wrists and legs to the four corners of the hospital bed, strapping them tightly. I lay helpless with only a thin gown as they shot me in the leg over and over again with syringes of I-didn't-know-what, but would later find out was a sedative. My actions were not those of a sane woman, and they were attempting to knock the instability out of me.

Instead, my visions continued even though my body lay limp. As I struggled to breathe, I was taken to the ICU to be monitored. One of the only things I can remember of that time was that I could not breathe and I wondered if I would die.

Yet I found myself alive. I lay, newly awake, in the midst of sheer hints of God's glory penetrating the window and finding me. Finding me! My greater-than-Gandalf had come and rescued me from terror and near death. He had come with an army to surround me. I saw God in the kind doctor who buttered my bread for the first food I would experience on this side of life. He was there in the young nurse's aide who washed me and braided my unkempt hair. God's presence, there, was triumph, the promise of hope, surely coming, surely mine.

Songs of Promise

As I pondered the meaning of the light of that Sunday morning, I was abruptly moved out of ICU and back to the mental ward. I breathed a sigh of relief as we moved past the eight-bed room where I had been before the ICU.

I was wheeled to a smaller room with two beds, and I was the only inhabitant. The old, dusty linoleum and white walls began to blunt the hope of that morning. I was beginning to sense a heaviness around me and in me. Questions haunted me.

What next? How will I get through this? How much damage did I cause my family?

The clock ticked and tocked as I tried to endure the day, eagerly anticipating the gift of my husband's daily visit. Jared brought my favorite cookies, *Csoki Zab Falatok*, oatmeal cookies with one side covered in chocolate. He brought my favorite meal, too, a pita filled with the fresh goodness of cabbage, cucumbers, tomatoes, rotisserie chicken, and creamy sauce from our favorite gyro stand, the one across the street from our home. It was a good sign that I wanted to eat again. I had lost my appetite in the sleepless nights of my episode.

Even more welcome than the food was the hope my husband ushered in to my mental wardroom in a heavenly way. After I ate, I lay on my bed and listened to the calm cadence of Jared's voice as he read from the Psalms. His voice reached my ears as a rich, poetic lyric with a profound melody I could feel in my bones.

As he read, the promises lifted from the page and anchored me in a faith I had cherished for nearly all my forty years of life. Each word felt weighty, beautiful. His voice stilled me as he read from Psalm 84, a passage beloved by my grandparents:

> How lovely is your dwelling place,
>   O LORD of hosts!
> My soul longs, yes, faints
>   for the courts of the LORD;
> my heart and flesh sing for joy
>   to the living God.
>
> Even the sparrow finds a home,
>   and the swallow a nest for herself,
>   where she may lay her young,

at your altars, O LORD of hosts,
  my King and my God.
Blessed are those who dwell in your house,
  ever singing your praise!

Blessed are those whose strength is in you,
  in whose heart are the highways to Zion.
As they go through the Valley of Baca
  they make it a place of springs;
  the early rain also covers it with pools.
They go from strength to strength;
  each one appears before God in Zion.
  (Ps. 84:1–7 ESV)

When he read of the "highways to Zion" and traveling from "strength to strength," I felt the tiniest hint of courage to trust for more.

Then, I closed my eyes and I rested. As Jared continued to read, I felt sweet repose wrapping around me, and I fell into a deep, dreamless sleep. I slept for only a few minutes, but oh, when I awoke! There was something solid in me. It filled me with emotion—substantive and real. It also gave me its name, sweetly, yet stronger than gold. It said, "I am hope."

And I knew. I just knew everything would be okay. There was yet a grand plan and purpose for my life. For Jared and me together. The knowledge called to me, told me to cling to this gorgeous, full-bodied thing: hope.

It came to me so beautifully in that anything-but-beautiful Hungarian hospital. It came with its defiant nature, a resolute champion of my story. It came in my size and shape, a reminder that the God of hope could be trusted as he had made me and knew me intimately, fully. It stood tall, telling me I could stand tall in the face of the tattered pieces that my life had become.

Before my manic episode, I had so many dreams that I believed I was ready to achieve. In the consuming despair, those dreams had looked like a tiny pile of ash. But here in a Hungarian mental ward, through his beloved Word, God spoke resilience and purifying fire and a victory in hope.

The True Nature of Hope

For the creation was subjected to futility, not willingly, but because of him who subjected it, in hope that the creation itself will be set free from its bondage to corruption and obtain the freedom of the glory of the children of God. (Rom. 8:20–21 ESV)

When I behold a wildflower and its resemblance to a salmon-colored flame, I think of this world my God has made. He has embedded hope in all we see. Although all that we see is "subjected to futility" and brokenness, still there is glory. This glory is pushing forth, in hope, against the bindings of futility that hold it for now, for a little while. The azure of a cloudless sky—with its radiant, saturating color—is the hope I am ever longing for, ever seeking.

Again, I want you to know that this hope is meant for you, too. I would not be writing this book if hope were not real. My life is proof of that hope.

Because of the language barrier, we still don't know precisely how close I came to death in that Hungarian ICU. Fifteen months later, in May 2016, I had to be hospitalized again after I banged my head repeatedly on a concrete wall while obeying the voices

I "heard" during another manic episode. Even though I survived both experiences, it was not certain I would come back to life as a fully functioning adult.

But I not only came back, I am now telling my story so that you can pick it up and read it. It is nothing less than a miracle that God has eradicated my shame and fear of speaking my story.

Hope. Oh, beloved friend, hope. It layers our sunrises in a million shades of color that become a living stream entering into our hearts. Hope proclaims a better word. Will you receive its glimmering light? Will you open yourself to the possibility of this hope "shining ever brighter" in you "till the full light of day" (Prov. 4:18)?

Hope is within us. We are imprinted with it, as is all of creation. After describing creation's futility, Romans 8 goes on to say, "For we know that the whole creation has been groaning together in the pains of childbirth until now. And not only the creation, but we ourselves, who have the firstfruits of the Spirit, groan inwardly as we wait eagerly for adoption as sons, the redemption of our bodies. For in this hope we were saved" (Rom. 8:22–24 ESV). There is an inward groaning down deep in the recesses of our souls, but this groaning is an affirmation of our true hope rather than a sign we are without hope. All around us, creation also groans with the same hope of the final redemption because everything made by God is inescapably imprinted with this same hope. We are meant to lead out with that hope and to display the hope we possess as part of "the firstfruits of the Spirit." For we are stewards of hope as the image-bearers of God within creation.

Every moment beckons us toward hope. In the five and a half years since my experience in that Hungarian mental ward, I have been reminded repeatedly to let hope grow from my heart and through my soul and be released so that all can see it. This moment-to-moment dependence on hope has brought me to where I am today.

Despair can seem as innocent as a sigh. But it can entice us to stop fighting for the light and to simply give in to the darkness. A sigh, then a cry, and on the exhale, we are entrenched in the opposite of hope.

In John Bunyan's classic story, *The Pilgrim's Progress*, Christian and his companion, Hopeful, fall asleep off "The Way," and are taken prisoner and beaten by Giant Despair, who feeds them many lies. He tells them to kill themselves because there is no hope.[2] But Christian is able to escape Giant Despair when he remembers that he has the "Key of Promise."[3]

So how do we, like Christian, escape despair?

First, we must take notice of our sighing. And then we must remember the faithfulness of God. In so doing, we receive the great grace of God. Our brokenness within and without is our fallen heritage, but we are healed through Christ. Then, our very next breath stokes the hope for which we are made. Hope is a flame we fan, a warm hearth we tend. Its intensity ushers in the sun of our days.

The End of Our Thoughts

When we struggle with mental illness, or any hardship, we struggle to keep hope alive in our thoughts, and the battle is often close. In ordinary moments of life, my insecurity bubbles up as I worry about the possibility of imminent attack. Then I hear a lie: "You are not enough to live your life." Or "You don't deserve love." Or a thousand other wretched calls that threaten to darken my thinking.

What do we do?

We must cling to our hope. Let it be that warm ember within our heart. Let it meet the promises of God calling it forth. Let the melody of song raise it to new heights.

We don't combat the darkness with our mental fists, punching out the would-be attackers of lying thoughts. No. We fill ourselves with the substance of our hope—Jesus. He is the all-sufficient one, the light in all the darkness, and he cannot be overcome.

We also take the time to know ourselves. For example, I know that about three or four in the afternoon, when I am with my children after school, is the time when I am likely to be attacked mentally. My mind will be flooded with a barrage of lies and an overwhelming sense of unworthiness. These times are most likely related to lingering feelings of guilt that I abandoned my kids in my hard days.

I know I must fight especially hard in these times, so I keep tried and true Scriptures readily available. "I have loved you with an everlasting love; I have drawn you with unfailing kindness" (Jer. 31:3). Or, "Trust in him at all times, O people; pour out your heart before him; God is a refuge for us" (Ps. 62:8 ESV). And so many more. I also ensure that a friend or a sister or other supporter is just a text or phone call away.

Despair wants us to think that our skies have already been determined. It wants us to believe we will always be overshadowed by dark clouds of shame, exhaustion over mental struggle, fear, or all the things that set themselves up against the truth of God within us.

But beloved, do not despair. Rather, hope.

I present my story as an aid to you, but my story, my words, and my pleading cannot fight for *your* life. Only you can do that. Hope is in you, for you, with you, but you must fight for it.

Even though you must take charge of your own battle, know that you have me and so many others who fight with you and for you. It's easy to get walled into our own prison cells and lose our perspective altogether. We must break through because we are meant for life, for exquisite hope.

Hope so often meets us at the end of ourselves, even at the end of our desire for existence, and surprises us by its utter tenacity. Just when we think despair will win, hope ignites again. Frederick Buechner eloquently expresses the perseverance of hope in *A Room Called Remember*:

> At last we see what hope is and where it comes from,
> hope as the driving power and outermost edge of faith.
> Hope stands up to its knees in the past and keeps its
> eyes on the future. There has never been a time past
> when God wasn't with us as the strength beyond our
> strength, the wisdom beyond our wisdom, as whatever
> it is in our hearts—whether we believe in God or not—
> that keeps us human enough at least to get by despite
> everything in our lives that tends to wither the heart
> and make us less than human.[4]

Yes, the best word, the Word made flesh, the hope of all the world, comes at last. Every time. And his hope does not lead us to futile places. When we lay hold of this indestructible hope it makes us new. We become the same stuff as our hope.

The Roots of Hope

The more we think about hope, the more we think about hope. Yes, you read that right. Hope breeds hope, and it is better than any medicine.

Please understand that I'm not downplaying the importance or effectiveness of medicine. Medicine has been so valuable to me. When I have tried to reduce it, even with a psychiatrist's consent on a trial basis, it has not gone well. I am very thankful for what is available to me today.

But there is no pill more powerful than hope.

Medicine gives us a fighting chance, but we are still in a battle. Hope takes us from surviving to thriving.

When I lay on that hospital bed in Szent Imre Kórház, sedated and near death, no one could predict what the rest of my life would be. Least of all me. The demonic lies I heard were so menacing, and they had become believable to me. The rest of my life could have been a quiet walk into the night as I sought to fend off the darkness enough to simply survive.

Enter hope. I can't recall what hope meant to me before all this. I knew I was supposed to have it, but I had no idea just how treasured and sustaining it could be.

Although Budapest is the most beautiful city I have ever beheld, when I lived there, the winters seemed endless, with damp, cold, dull skies nearly matching the tall cement apartment buildings. Life without hope is like living under those skies permanently. Like going through the motions of living without seeing light breaking through or the rich color of sky or the rising and ebbing colors of the sun.

Hope gives us wings to fly into a bright sky. "Now faith is confidence in what we hope for and assurance about what we do not see" (Heb. 11:1). Hope holds hands with our faith. For me, it resurrected the belief that though my dreams were ashen, there were yet days, even great days, to live.

I am not the first to speak of hope in this way. In the first century the Apostle Paul wrote, "We rejoice in our sufferings, knowing that suffering produces endurance, and endurance produces character, and character produces hope, and hope does not put us to shame, because God's love has been poured into our hearts through the Holy Spirit who has been given to us" (Rom. 5:3–5 ESV).

I had suffered greatly, and so had those whom I loved most. Yet, Paul promises that suffering brings strength, endurance, and rich character, which lead to hope. And this hope brings the limitless reality of God's love poured like molten gold into our hearts through the Comforter given by Jesus himself. Nothing, absolutely nothing, of our foul enemy or our fallen inheritance can stand against that hope and love.

This same hope can change our entire perspective. I love that Paul says we will not be "put to shame" by hope. Because the awful truth is that there is so much shame related to mental illness, especially within the church, and especially for those involved in leadership or active ministry. But hope is absolutely standing against this shame. I saw resolutely that I could rise up and stand strong in hope, against the shame, and share my story.

In this hope, I also purpose to do more. I want to offer its brightness as the truth radiating through my story—and your story. It is like a candle that cannot be snuffed out calling to our God-given light. Hope dwells with his Holy Spirit that dwells in us, and this hope will not disappoint. No, it will be like his glorious light, the one whose brilliance overcomes the darkness, every time.

All this light changes everything, doesn't it? None of us need to dwell under dark, colorless skies. Instead, we can run under skies saturated in the colors of life. We can rest under the sun in lush gardens of ripe fruit, ready for our tasting. We can see. Really see. And we can come to life because the light is meant for us. Sighs of despair disappear into the dark void, never to be heard again.

This is what I see for you, friend. I have been so privileged to walk this path from darkness to light over these past five-plus years. God's sure, gentle, persistent voice is beckoning—can you hear it? Can you see the glorious hope he is promising?

Oh, I pray that you can. How deeply I want to take your hand and walk toward the dawn God planned just for you.

3

THE OPENNESS OF THE MORNING
From Endings to Beginnings

April 2015

I hunched in a swivel chair in an upstairs bedroom in the house where we were living in Souderton, Pennsylvania. Mary, my counselor, was speaking to me, and I was trying to focus on her words while gazing out at the backside of a church and its cemetery where I often walked in the late afternoons.

This mission house, where we had stayed for several months before our move to Hungary in May 2012, had been our soft place to land when we returned in March 2015. It was a warm and cozy gift, given simply and beautifully. One of our mission-supporting churches had told us we could use it for as long as we needed and had lovingly prepared it for us when we moved back to the States after those days of my major manic episode and my hospitalization.

I sought to understand, even in some small way, the nature of my grief. In the month since we had returned to Pennsylvania,

I had felt smothered in a constant haze under a rain-dreary sky. Pervasive emotional pain was my constant companion.

Mary was describing to me different elements of grief (or DAYS of grief)—denial, anger, yearning, and sadness—and explaining how we cycle through these emotions as we move toward acceptance. Normally a heart-on-my-sleeve kind of girl, I realized I didn't understand what I was feeling at the moment. The inescapable numbness frightened me.

It certainly wasn't my first encounter with loss or grief. Periods of grief were scattered across my life like shards of broken glass. When I was a child, my family had lost our dairy farm. Later, I felt the particular anguish of a heart broken into a million pieces when I lost a romantic love. Then my mother was diagnosed with cancer and taken from all of us despite a long, valiant battle. My season of mourning for my mother had never ended, but there had been a sense of closure in her death.

But these post-Budapest days were different because there were so many endings all at once. It was like the sudden tearing away of the fabric of my life, which I could never grasp again. I had even lost my mother's engagement ring—the one she arranged for me to receive when she was dying of cancer. The ring, an irreplaceable reminder of my mother's love and faithfulness for more than a dozen years, had been stolen while I was in the Hungarian hospital. So much of what I valued in life was just gone.

We had been ripped away from many dear people and beloved places, destroying a dream and a purpose we had been cultivating for a decade, since Jared and I had first interned in Hungary in the summer of 2005. We returned to Hungary in the summers of 2008 and 2010, introducing our new babies to these precious friends who had become like family. Finally, we decided to move to Hungary, arriving in Budapest in May 2012 after two years of preparation for our long-term commitment. We spent the next three years learning the language, loving the people, immersing our children in that same language and culture, and ministering to students all over Hungary. Leaving Hungary, leaving that mission field, destroyed the most significant ministry dream we had as a family. Our expectations of rich, beautiful experiences for years to come had all been left behind.

This appalling lack of closure increased the crushing burden I carried. My mental breakdown had cost me so much, and the ones I loved the most—who were simply innocent bystanders—were paying an intolerably high price for my weakness. How could I possibly find my way through this grief? The many questions I raised to God and others elicited only silence.

Friends and family had come and gone from our beloved Budapest home during our last days there—while I tried to sleep again. A small portion of friends found their way to our flat to say goodbye in the seven days between my release from the hospital and our return to the States. Through it all, I had felt severed from my life, unable to process, living as someone else, someone strange. All seemed wrong to us and to many of those we were leaving behind. There was no roadmap for this journey of anguish of spirit and heart and mind and soul amid the sudden goodbyes. I could only pray to hang onto the good, millisecond by millisecond, and to keep breathing. The endings, too numerous, wreaked havoc over every coping mechanism I knew as I processed my grief.

A mere month later, I sat in a Pennsylvania bedroom with Mary, trying to come to terms with what I had left behind.

The Messiness of Grief

In the movie *We Are Marshall*, a character who lost his son in a plane crash, which killed seventy-five people associated with the Marshall University football team, says simply, "Grief is messy."[1] In the film, this character had lost his wife and then his son, an only child, and he appeared simply angry and hard. But there was more. Within his heart lay sadness and also love, which could not die even as he and the entire community dealt with various complex emotions and actions.

Grief is messy. So how do any of us make any sense of it?

One way to think of grief is as a mess of tangled yarn of various colors. The competing emotions are each their own hue, but they twist in and out with one another. The only way to find our way through our grief is to work our way through this tangled ball of emotion. We may want to examine one of the threads, for example a coral strand, which is actually a joy-filled, beautiful memory. But as we yank on that coral strand, we find it also brings up a midnight blue one, representing profound sadness, because the place and people of that beautiful, coral memory are now lost to us.

For me, this intermingling of the joy of hopeful beginnings and the pain of grief-filled endings are drawn out most sharply in memories of Speakout English Camp. This camp is held each summer in Keszthely, Hungary, when students from all over Hungary come for a weeklong experience of learning English. Jared and I spent six summers there. We were there before we had kids, and eventually with each of our three kids. We served as a family there, sharing the life-changing message of Jesus with Hungarian students.

We also experienced a spirit of togetherness there with some of the dearest people we've ever known. With them we created and participated in fun activities, took long walks by the lake, fed ducks, roamed palace gardens, and enjoyed Hungarian ice cream called *fagyi*. In a camp-wide activity called Staff Hunt, we dressed up and "hid" ourselves around town, looking goofy while the campers tried to find us in a café or fishing by the lake. For years, I called Speakout my "happy place."

Then I fell into a tragic downward spiral and we had to leave it all behind. For years, there was a hard, hot ball in my chest whenever I thought about Speakout. Even today, memories can still burn. So many rivers of heartache lying deep inside my emotions cut new canals through places of my soul I didn't even know existed.

But as much as I wanted to run from this grief, to further numb my pain with television, or movies, or romance novels, the only thing I could truly do was sit with it. I lifted up a simple cry, "Oh God, why?"

Anyone who has grieved at all knows this question very often remains unanswered, at least for a time. Yet, it is still important to ask such a thing because our questions mean we are making room for the profound ache of it all.

Even years after my mental illness forced us to leave Hungary, I have very few answers to the "God, why?" question. I still feel a soul-filling ache at the prospect of never returning to Speakout. I still cry out in anguish at what mental illness did to me and does to so many.

Grief is messy. Yet, only by remaining in that grief can we ever be free to live again, live anew. Only when we remain in it can we authentically tell our story. Only when we remain in it can we can give voice to the redeeming love of God.

My Grief Has a Name

When Mary worked with me in the spring of 2015 on the emotions of my grief, it all felt like too much. My spirit was resisting the work of entering the agony of my heart. It felt like the security of my life had been ripped from me with great finality, and I was now standing at the edge of a precipice and being asked to jump without a safety harness. Panic and weakness vied for control of my heart.

But I had to take the step from the seeming safety of my solid ground of numbness. Only then could I begin to name my grief. And naming my grief could help me find the courage to deal with its near-lethal effects on my life.

What do I mean by "naming grief"? To name our grief is to give voice to our loss. It can be very hard to do because we must acknowledge the place of our pain, which can make us feel utterly out of control. It can plunge us into darkness.

Although there are many things I miss about our home in Hungary and my life before my mental breakdown, there is one overarching thread to my grief that I can identify: the total loss of my reputation. Although my image was imperfect before, in the time of the wildness of my mental illness, I became openly incoherent, catatonic, and delusional. There was no pretending I didn't display these things, shocking as they were. With this fall from grace, I felt as though any path forward was overshadowed by a creeping darkness. How would I ever become someone more than a woman covered in the questionable fog of an unstable mind?

But I *have* found a path forward. Now, I can grieve this loss and weep the tears of shame because I know God wants to dry every one. I can pour out my heart that has been broken by lost relationships, those who could not meet me on the other side of my mental breakdown. I can mourn all the events I thought I would be able to experience, all the services I thought I would be able to give while living as a missionary to Hungary. Naming grief does not make it easy, but it does point us to the deep places of our souls instead of allowing us to cover up the wounds by numbing through substance abuse, binge-watching a TV show, or returning too quickly into busyness.

As I have continued to learn, I realize that I must sit with this stark, painful thing I don't understand. I'm not alone in this. At some point, most of us will find ourselves in a similar situation. Instead of trying to escape it, we must remain. As we remain, we find the courage to jump off that precipice toward a dark unknown of grief, and we discover that the tender, compassionate hands of God hold us.

We cannot feel those hands when we stand in place, stuck in the muddy ground, where we rely on other things to distract us from our grief. We cannot experience the full embrace of God when we are numbing ourselves from our pain. No, we can only experience the demonstration of God's love through the leap and the exercise of trust. Here we can understand the lamenting, empathetic, compassionate, and boundless heart of God. He is ever ready to embrace us in the nakedness of our pain.

As we name our grief, we can grieve with purpose although the pain very well may become stronger for a time. Yet, like localized wounds, when our places of grief are exposed, they can thus be healed to the very deepest parts. Full healing may take many years—even until we are home with God forever. However, we gain greater hope at each place where we allow God, in full sight of his love, to touch us in our mourning.

It's a Process

In all honesty, my healing is only happening now as I write these words, more than five years after my breakdown and hospitalization that forced us to leave Hungary. It has taken me this long to come wholeheartedly to the place where I can deal with the torturous nights of my loss. I tell you this because I want you to know that it is okay if your grief journey also takes a significant amount of time.

Our grief journey is very complex, and the nearly apocalyptic fallout of mental illness can be a great force of destruction. For so many of us, our illness has devastating effects on those we love most. How do we begin to deal with the grief that our low times have caused for others?

Surprisingly, the best contribution we can make to their healing is seeking healing for ourselves. We must not allow pain upon pain, shame upon shame, heaping upon heaping of guilt. When we see our strength renewed, our hope born again, and God's love salving our deepest hurt, we will gain the resilience to walk with our loved ones in their grief. Healing for us begets healing for them.

My husband Jared says this about his journey:

> I experienced the lowest points of my life as I saw my
> best friend, my beloved wife, in a manic episode, and
> I couldn't recognize her. The trauma was very real for
> me. Then, to be in the ICU in Hungary not knowing

how this story would end—this brought me to a crisis of faith. I asked, "Was God really good, and could I trust that he was with us?"

As we came back to the States, after three months, Abby's psychiatrist told us the progress in her healing in such a short time was a miracle. I saw the steadfastness of the Lord in Abby as she faced her fears with courage and shared her story. Then I realized I, too, was experiencing healing. And I began to ask the questions: "Can the Lord save me, too, from my fears, my shame?" The answer is a resounding yes!

These are humbling words to hear. My husband saw me walk an intensely personal path toward gaining my physical, emotional, and spiritual strength. Yet, he can say that my journey toward new beginnings, the wholeness after the brokenness, is in many ways, his too.

No matter how long or short a process is, none of us relish the thought of being *in process*. My Western mindset draws me to a linear point of view: Races have a winner, and I must win. To win, I must be the fastest and reach the end ahead of all others. Not only is it impossible to rush to the end of grief, but this hurry-up-and-get-there approach can easily defeat us before we even begin.

When dealing with grief related to mental illness, the healing process is complicated because we are prone to vicious cycles of thinking. Self-loathing in particular can become so great that we are pulled into relapse or toward anything we can find to ease these feelings. This is all to the detriment of what we most need—grace for our brokenness.

In this process, our perspective initially feels inky black to murky gray, as if the darkness will swallow us whole. Yet, the clarity of Jesus breaks through as he calls to us with outstretched arms. He is the light for this darkness we are walking through because for this he died. We will find him as we journey through the darkness because we walk toward a fuller understanding of his love. For his heart has borne grief, for us and this world. The prophet Isaiah calls him "a man of sorrows and acquainted with grief" (Isa. 53:3 ESV). And more than food or drink or the air we breathe, it is the rich depth of his love, reaching through the darkness, that sustains us.

In receiving his love, we come to realize why we must remain for a time in the place of our grief: there is no other way to truly come to know Jesus. After all the hell of my states of delusions and full-blown psychosis, it was impossible for me to gain the strength to tell my story for all to read. That is, it would have been impossible without the love of Jesus touching every place of agonizing pain, of undying sorrow—the grief spawned from my worst days of living.

Henri Nouwen expresses well this process toward the healing of our grief:

> We hear an invitation to allow our mourning to become a place of healing, and our sadness a way through pain to dancing. Who is it Jesus said would be blessed? "Those who mourn" (Matt 5:4 NIV). We learn to look fully into our losses, not evade them. By greeting life's pain with something other than denial we may find something unexpected. By inviting God into our difficulties we ground life—even its sad

moments—in joy and hope. When we stop grasping our lives we can finally be given more than we could ever grab for ourselves. And we learn the way to a deeper love for others.[2]

Affirming how important it is to not run away from our grief, Nouwen also invites us to see our grief as connecting—not separating—us to others. As we stay present with our grief, we join the ache of all of humanity for a better world. We realize that we are not the only ones in process and that this dying world manifests the grief of all through the ages. When we enter this cry of all who have ever lived, there is only one place we can go. We cry with Simon Peter, "Lord, to whom shall we go? You have the words of eternal life" (John 6:68 ESV). He is the life-giver, the wellspring of unending beauty, and as the great Russian writer Dostoyevsky famously said, "Beauty saves the world."[3]

When we see the larger purpose of our grief, we can lament in community over greater pain. Thus we enter a communal experience meant to heal a broken world. Psalm 130 shows this beautifully:

> Out of the depths I cry to you, LORD;
>   LORD, hear my voice.
> Let your ears be attentive
>   to my cry for mercy. (Ps. 130:1–2)

Then, as we step outside of ourselves, we are moved to compassion for all who are hurting. We see this in the progression of Psalm 130:

> I wait for the LORD, my whole being waits,
>   and in his word I put my hope.

> I wait for the LORD
>> more than watchmen wait for the morning,
>> more than watchmen wait for the morning.
> Israel, put your hope in the LORD,
>> for with the LORD is unfailing love
>> and with him is full redemption.
> He himself will redeem Israel
>> from all their sins. (Ps. 130:6–8)

As the psalmist makes the honest journey of his anguish, he is moved to hope as a watchman awaiting God's redemption. Then his watching flows into a call to all of Israel, encouraging his people to hope in God because of his love for and rescue of them.

When we truly travel the process of grief, we find we gain far more than we could ever have imagined, for we gain the heart of God. On the other hand, if we choose not to embrace the journey of our pain, we are left hardened and embittered with mountain-sized chips on our shoulders. I have learned that reality from my own journey, from the times I didn't grieve well.

Find comfort in the process. It is not a race to win but a grace to receive. As long as you are true to what lies in your grief, you will become grounded by solid, enduring things. You will find the love of Jesus, whose infinite pain named him that "man of sorrows" (Isa. 53:3 ESV). We are in the best company, then, on this long road home, because he is able to heal—he plans to heal us forever and ever—and we can fully trust him for this.

Begin Again with Others

I was scared and a little bit excited as we traveled along Interstate 95 with a U-Haul trailer hitched to our gold 2005 minivan. Five months after our sudden return from Hungary, we were en route from Pennsylvania to a yearlong internship with our mission organization in Orlando, Florida. These months of upheaval and the dreaded "in-between" led to this two-day road trip. We had first contemplated this step while we were yet in Hungary but were unsure if we would be accepted to the program or if we would want to remain in missions and/or with this organization.

But now it seemed like a great fit. Designed for people of every life stage who were in a significant time of transition, we believed the internship would provide an amazing opportunity for healing and growth. Many of the other participants were transitioning back to the United States from overseas, just like us.

But I was pretty sure they were not "just like us."

As we entered life with others, I was haunted by the idea that I was wearing some sort of scarlet letter, something that marked me as belonging to the "clinically unstable" group. I longed for relationship and to begin true relationships with others. But was I ready? How could I really begin again when I was unsure of so much about myself? And how could people really know me unless I told them all about my bipolar disorder and what it had done to me and to those I love? Many of us can find ourselves in this unsure place if we've suffered the grief of losing a spouse or a child, or our quality of life as we deal with chronic illness, or any number of events that end life as we have known it.

As life unfolded in this new environment, I slowly came to realize I was doing the work of grieving the messy endings of things so that I could become ready to begin anew. Many in this program were mourning the loss of overseas homes and places, so I wasn't alone. On my good days, I was certain they were all my long-lost best friends. On my hard days, I would envy them because they had planned their departures in advance and so had a sense of closure that my family and I did not enjoy.

In this time, I also received a mentor, Alex, who had special understanding of my journey with mental illness and being forced to leave an overseas home suddenly. Our times of fellowship and friendship were rich, but I was still raw with grief and would easily take offense whether speaking about medicines or symptoms with her. She received it all with so much grace that gradually, through this pivotal relationship, I began to trust again, something I had not been able to do since our final days in Budapest had devastated some of my dearest relationships, as I will discuss more in Chapter Five.

In mental illness or similar conditions, shame is often heaped on those who, in their illness, do bizarre things. For me, I felt a lot of shame because an important relationship did not survive my mania.

But I learned how to speak into my dark night of grief upon grief, guilt upon guilt, and shame upon shame, and say, "No more!" I have heard these words echoing from my Savior as I process the messiness of the endings I mourn.

This year of relationship, this internship, provided an environment where I was safe to land just as I was. I quickly learned that many here were very different from others who had hurt me acutely. They were safe and protective of my heart. Although trust and opening up were still hard at times, we all lived in the same apartment complex so our community was close in multiple ways.

I found great beauty in moms talking while kids rode bikes and played. My heart filled as my three-year-old, six-year-old, and eight-year-old made new friends after they had been forced to say so many sorrowful goodbyes. These beginnings called for celebration after near-death and heart-rending grief.

A month after beginning the internship and only six months after my hospitalization in Hungary, I shared more of my story with my small group. My new, and already dear, friend Keda said, "Abby, I know you have been through all this and you have something called 'bipolar,' but I just want to say, you are one of the healthiest people I know." Her words meant everything to me and acted as a healing balm for my battered soul, serving as just one of many blessings of new beginnings in a healthy, restorative community.

In saying this, Keda meant that I knew well who I was. Also, I knew the things that could lead me down mentally, emotionally, and spiritually unhealthy paths. As I received her affirmation, I realized, deep within, that I had this knowledge because I had taken the time to grieve the endings. I looked full in the face my years of not knowing or not being willing to admit my struggles to myself or anyone else. We had been living in Hungary for a few months when Samuel, our third child, was born. I fell into a deep depression and spent days upon days of taking care of him and reading Christian romance novels and no more. In my fear and shame, I wouldn't get help.

Mental illness is not the fault of the one who suffers that illness. But we are responsible for knowing how we are broken by the effects of mental illness. We need to engage in healthy grief and really deal with the fallout of our illness in order to move toward wholeness.

I speak truthfully, but tenderly. We need to be kind to ourselves in our grief processes, receiving the grace of a God who fights passionately for our best. We must spend time in God's presence, receiving his unconditional love like a gentle, encompassing embrace. His intentional care and heart for us comes to surprise and sustain in the sweetest of ways, calling all sorrow home to his heart of ultimate healing. I needed this perspective to move from endings to beginnings.

We all need that insight and outlook. We need to gaze upon those great vistas of that faithful orb of light rising upon a battle scene, with our enemy completely defeated. We need to stand with hands held high, ready, for a new day.

The Beginning That Will Never End

Tension persists because grief remains with us even amid the new mercies each day brings. To be healed means we reach new places of light and beauty in our souls; yet the pain from the darkness lingers. So, we are constantly navigating between worlds of dark and light. But the rising sun will have the final say, as does the God of that sun.

I especially need to cling to this perspective when I seek to understand the fallout of my major manic episodes. One of the symptoms of my manic episode in Hungary is clinically called "grandiose delusions."[4] In the most intense moments of my delusions, my mind was filled with scenes from the prophetic writings of Revelation and Daniel, prophecies of the end times. This means that in my hard days, I hear lies on cataclysmic levels. Something as simple and brutal as: "Jesus will not win in the end." I have felt weak to be subject to such a penetration of evil.

In the years since my hospitalization in Hungary, I have remembered a lesson I first learned during my college days: when our great enemy tips his hand, it is our key to victory. In other words, when he attempts to get me to disbelieve in Jesus, I recognize him for the liar he is and embrace the truth, which defeats the lie. It is in this place of realization that I remember the beginning of all things.

The world in Genesis 1 is perfect. Gorgeous. Vivid beyond our wildest dreams. Vibrant colors in azure sky, emerald sea, mossy grass, cherry red, apple green, redwood tree, striped tiger and zebra. All called good by a good God. Man and woman, crowns of creation, the focal point of God's covenant love.

Then, the serpent seductively and cunningly whispers, "Did God really say . . . ?" (Gen. 3:1). Razor sharp arrow of lie about what? That Eve wasn't beautiful? That Adam wasn't a good man? That the fruits God gave weren't delicious? No. So crafty was he that he spoke as Eve's ally, as if he wanted to give her the ultimate gift: becoming like God. In so doing, the evil one planted the seed of doubt about God's goodness and love.

Eve was like God, made in his image. She had perfect communion with God, Adam, and all that was. But she was tempted, led astray, through the lie that God was not all good and that what was momentary, right before her, was better. So, perfection was shattered. All hatred, envy, strife, and a million other forces of darkness entered the world.

How could such a beautiful beginning end so tragically? But this state of fallenness wasn't really the end. Even in the garden, God spoke of one who would come from Eve and crush the head of the serpent (Gen. 3:15). Redemption. Every bit of the tragic fall of the world bought back.

History has been marching forth toward this full redemption, this beginning, which will have no end. Jesus has come to give all a new day, forever, a sunrise to color everything for all time and eternity. On this beginning, I call you to gaze, reorienting your perspective toward the light shining brighter and brighter. This light is the one I've already mentioned. The one that can never, ever be overcome.

4

WARM HUES BECKON
From Exile to Homecoming

October 2013

The everyday pressure to be a worthy wife and good mother led me once again into the kitchen. My task was simple: finish chopping the onions for my homemade salsa. But I simply couldn't finish because my hands were shaking too much. I gripped the countertop to try and make the sensation pass while my mind was flooded with thoughts, negative thoughts. It felt like I was spiraling down a funnel of thought, with only destruction ahead. I needed help. But oh how afraid I was of my inner state and the judgment I mercilessly reflected back on my already battered spirit. I dared not share my struggle with anyone because I was sure their judgment would break me.

Later, when I had gained more self-awareness after my 2015 hospitalization, I could trace these episodes that impaired my ability to even chop onions back to the summer of 2013, when I had stopped taking my prescribed antidepressants. The precarious nature of my mental health during this time was compounded by the fact that I was avoiding seeing a psychiatrist or even a family doctor regularly. These decisions led me into a lonely wilderness. My deep longing from those days could be summed up by Eva Hoffman in her memoir, *Lost in Translation:* "We want to be home in our tongue. We want to be able to give voice accurately and fully to ourselves and our sense of the world."[1] I was an exile who had lost my voice, my sense of worth, and—therefore—my place in the world. I became a stranger to myself and, gradually, to others.

The loneliness of the wilderness does something to you. If you're there too long, you begin to look for strength on your own. This will lead you even further away to the feeling of utter desolation, dust, and dry rivers. If you are like me, you try to eat the food of "capability" and drink from the river called "performance." Yet, you find no nourishment there, only judgment and a bereft spirit. Oh, how we need the living water of the grace of God. But oh, how we doubt that it is for us.

Our Wilderness Experience

Being human in this world means we spend at least some of our time wandering in the desert, east of God's perfect Eden. Throughout the Bible, God tested his people in the wilderness, "to know what was in [their hearts]" (Deut. 8:2). He wanted them to seek him above all others, to hunger and thirst for him as David did in the wilderness of Judah (Ps. 63:1), as Jesus in the wilderness of Judea (Matt. 4:1–11).

Yet, so much of the time, instead of receiving the manna God gave, his people longed for the land of their slavery, Egypt. They wasted their wilderness, wanting everything but God, the only one who could truly satisfy.

In the fall of 2013, I wanted to want God, I really did. Yet so much of my wandering came because I longed even more for the perfect image—to be seen as capable and put together. And God was not to be found there. Tim Keller reminds me of this truth when he says,

> Home, then, is a powerful but elusive concept. The strong feelings that surround it reveal some deep longing within us for a place that absolutely fits and suits us, where we can be, or perhaps find, our true Selves. Yet it seems that no real place or actual family ever satisfies these yearnings, though many situations arouse them.[2]

Our longing for home seems to promise only disappointment. As we are delivered into exile, we can wonder if God really cares about us, if he is truly for us. In this gap between longing and fulfillment, we must find our way to God. Yet, the great revelation is that two thousand years ago, he made his way to us.

In order to better understand our longing and how God means to meet it, we have to go deeper into the pain of our brokenness.

For me, this brokenness was bound up in mental illness, which brooded within me. But I had no idea how to really enter my own pain related to the undiagnosed bipolar disorder, which I carried around. I knew, in part, it meant I had to find a way to trust others to get past the damning judgment I believed I would receive for my failure to live up to their expectations. This sentiment shouted to me from the depths of my own self-condemnation.

A Needed Friend

As things got worse, I needed a trusted friend, someone who would receive my vulnerable, not-together self. One day, I finally opened up to our team leader, Virág, who had known me since 2006, when we met during my first internship in Hungary. It had been hard for us to meet regularly for a few months, but at our fall retreat, I finally sat face-to-face with her and met her compassionate eyes. It was clear that I needed to be honest with her and myself about how poorly I was feeling.

It was hard to talk about, but I told her what had happened recently when I took my four-year-old daughter, Susie, to see a doctor. Virág listened as I explained, as best I could, the fear that invaded me as I stood on the bus, hanging on to the handle above me for dear life. My heart was pounding in my chest, and I felt sure I would faint. I had wondered if Susie, vulnerable and cute as could be, would be safe or able to get me help if I collapsed. Sharing this vulnerable moment with Virág was a breakthrough moment for me where my mental health troubles were exposed.

Virág listened patiently with great care and silently processed what she heard and then reached out to her husband and other members of the team. Although I knew they each loved me genuinely, I was terrified of the judgment I would receive upon my ability to be a wife, mother, and missionary.

Our mentors and leaders let Jared pull back from ministry and gave us space to receive counseling. We will forever be thankful for that brief respite, although our gratitude can at times be marred by the knowledge that an unwillingness to face my mental illness remained.

It baffles me now. Why couldn't I see that something was truly wrong? Why does this happen to so many of us on the mental illness journey? My only answer is that the days of our wilderness have not harvested the fullness of our need. There is the need for a desperation that brings us to a place of humility where we are willing to admit our struggle. We still hunger and thirst for what won't satisfy and feel the fear of discovery. Oh that fear! We have our eyes on the giants and the strength of the enemy, as did the Israelite spies of old. We believe too little in the full rescue and plan of God.

But I don't want to do now what I have too often done—beat myself up for my actions or inactions. Rather, I now have the eyes to see that I needed every day in the wilderness to prepare to receive the promised land of God. In those Budapest days, I was still in exile.

The Essence of Exile

Exile is inextricably linked to our fallen inheritance. After Adam and Eve sinned, all perfection was broken, and they could no longer be fully in God's presence. God banished them and "placed on the east side of the Garden of Eden cherubim and a flaming sword flashing back and forth to guard the way to the tree of life" (Gen. 3:24). The following centuries of Adam and Eve's long, long lives were lived in exile. Toil for work. Hard times in giving birth. Disparity in their relationship, as Eve desired Adam and he lorded it over her (Gen. 3:15–18). One of their sons murdering another. They were desperately lost to the perfection of their birthplace, their home—this is the truest nature of exile.

"Exile and homecoming" is one of the great themes of the Bible.[3] It's a narrative that paints our stories in large brushstrokes.

And it casts itself across our vision as we wander, stumble, walk, and—yes—run toward our forever home with God. With our experience of exile come these tiny particles, like sand, which sting our eyes and cause great irritation or even blindness.

So, how do we see our way through this?

As I was walking recently and listening to a Tim Keller podcast, I heard him say, "We cannot survive *with* the wilderness. We cannot survive *without* the wilderness."[4] God did not banish Adam and Eve out of hatred, but love. He knew that it was only in experiencing their need that they could ever find their way to true relationship with God again.

Friends, our exile is never without purpose. Living within the wilderness brings constant learning about who we truly are—both as the beloved of God and as his creature, uniquely made by him. For me, life in exile involves a mental illness journey; yet, I am fully in the staying, keeping, guarding, protecting hand of God. The wilderness can bring each of us to a state of coming, moment-by-trusting-moment, home to God.

Beyond the Mirage

In the days, months, and years after my dark time in Budapest and another episode in Orlando fifteen months later, I realized I had been searching for things to replace God. Call them idols. These idols included beauty, notoriety as a writer or speaker, how well I performed my responsibilities, and more. I fell down to worship every mirage in my wilderness, seeking satisfaction.

I don't embrace this realization in order to beat up my already battered self. Rather, it is an act of surrender that provides a blueprint for understanding those changing skies, my ever-shifting perspectives, which might also help you understand yours. In full-blown times of exile, we get a mirage of fulfillment when we insist on choosing our way through the wilderness. We build our own roads toward our own destinations over the course of our entire lives. But they all have to be torn down if we are ever going to find our way to our true home.

As I look back on my days before the hospital in Budapest, I shudder. All around me pretty things were seeking my attention, luring me to a seeming promised land. Yet, they might very well have destroyed me and my family. There were temptations toward fame and fulfillment that could have completely unmoored me.

But we can learn to see life beyond the pleasant things, the pretty things, the shiny, sparkly things. When we are tested to the very core, we can come to know our true north, our anchoring sun. My treacherous road of mental illness has nearly killed me more than once, but I actually bear in my heart a thankfulness for every facet of it.

When we journey beyond the seductive baubles, we find the true colors, true food and drink, true sustainment that God wants to give us. We find our sunrise, the things we are meant to know, and the truths we are meant to live out. We find them because we realize our greatest desire, our greatest need, is God himself, not anything he could give us.

We readily say that God is the only one we need. So why must we go through so many hard things to realize the truth of that statement? Because there is a cost to fully gaining that understanding: we must die. Not literally, but in every other way. We must die to our desires, dreams, reputation, self-reliance. We must die to the very essence of the ways we make ourselves exist outside of God.

The gift, then, of a journey with mental illness is the gut-wrenching process that unmasks our self-sufficiency. Our limitations are laid bare, and we suffer the death of all we hope to be by ourselves. We see the corpse of everything we had hoped to make of our lives lying there, limp on the ground. But when we look up—oh—when we look up! We can then see the arms we have longed for outstretched over the cerulean blue of the desert sky. They reach for us over warm shades of hilly sand and enter right to the longing, wanting cry of our souls for God.

It bears repeating that I never want to be seen as dealing lightly or tritely with mental illness. It is a ferocious beast in the hands of evil, which longs to consume us. But within mental illness is a great paradox that only the God who became one with our frailty can create. Our mental illness is a part of the "easy and light" burden Jesus promises to give us when we come to him in our weariness and heavily burdened selves (Matt. 11:28–30). He has the power to change the landscape and sky, the full vista of our lives, and he longs to do just this. As we survive our living hells, he longs to heal. He desires to replace all we have lost with the great value that we find in him. He is the most real of all, the anti-mirage, and the utter depth of our truest vision.

A Surprising Promise in the Wasteland

July 2016

Jared and I were out to dinner, at a table for two. It was our thirteenth wedding anniversary and one worth celebrating. I was alive despite all that had sought to kill me. Just a few weeks earlier, I had mentally unraveled again, ending up in a mental ward for the second time in fifteen months. My sleep was only beginning to regulate, and my terror-filled visions had just recently receded.

My beloved in every way, Jared handed me a card with words from Isaiah 51:11, describing "the ransomed of the LORD" returning to Zion with "everlasting joy . . . upon their heads" (ESV). How stunning, how beautiful, how promise-filled! A bold declaration of exiles returning home. The words felt right from heaven's hand. Despite the terror and acute pain, home was coming and, by God, the whole ransomed lot of us would see it.

How do we really, truly begin to believe that God is going to heal so fully that all our pain will be a distant memory? To press a little deeper, how do we begin to believe that healing is our inheritance, which is attainable and available here on this wrecked earth—not just when we are home in heaven one day?

A mentality laced with shame is handed to those on a mental illness journey. This perspective is served up on a tarnished silver platter as if it is the only earthly destiny of someone going through mental illness. I won't blame any one sector of society for this view of people with mental illness; it is simply what is offered in a fallen world that lacks the hope of a here-and-now redemption of the lives of God's beloved. On one end of the continuum is a secular view that says therapy and medicine will be the complete solution. On the other end, too often, are Christians who seem to say some prayer and Bible study are all that is truly needed.

But God. He is rich in mercy (Eph. 2:4), and he is offering a better word. He offers his grace and, in all things, longs to heal us, bring us home. He doesn't tell us to put our faith in medicine, although he offers it as a tool that has greatly helped many, myself included. He also doesn't tell us to *try harder* to rid ourselves of dark thoughts and faulty ways of viewing ourselves and our lives.

No. He does for us now as he did for all humanity two thousand years ago. He takes on flesh and becomes to us, "Immanuel, God with us" (Matt. 1:23). In this, he promises to be with us in the deep waters so they will not overwhelm us. He is with us in the fire, declaring we will not be burned (Isa. 43:2), and we will be like Shadrach, Meshach, and Abednego, who were not consumed in the fiery furnace during their exile in Babylon but were saved by a man in dazzling white (Daniel 3). He does it all because we are precious and honored, and he loves us (Isa. 43:4).

We find in the truth of the incarnation of God that we who are in every way exiled from our first home find our way back. We lift our eyes and behold our Immanuel, who made a way home in the midst of the harshest of wildernesses. We trust in his goodness and believe his arms long to hold us in all the wretchedness of our wildernesses. And in that holding, we believe he longs to do a work beyond our wildest imagination, which will give us strength to rise up and enter the fruitful, secure place he has for us.

As I meditated on Isaiah 51:13, I looked up the passage and found verse three of the same chapter. This verse has transformed the way I view my life and brought me home, back to his heart and away from my exile mentality.

> For the LORD comforts Zion; he comforts all her waste
> places and makes her wilderness like Eden, her desert
> like the garden of the LORD; joy and gladness will
> be found in her, thanksgiving and the voice of song.
> (Isa. 51:3 ESV)

We are each Zion, as we believe in Jesus. We are his bride, his truest love; therefore, this verse is a love song to us. We can cling as tightly to these words as our deepest selves long to, never being afraid they are meant for someone else or are somehow not true. To underscore how we are being brought home, we hear that our wilderness will be made like Eden. This promise harkens to the heritage of our first home and is a symbol, therefore, of our restoration to it.

Maybe you still think God means this promise for our life in heaven, not our life here. But Jesus said, "In this world you will have trouble. But take heart! I have overcome the world" (John 16:33). He has overcome, and through him, we overcome. We will struggle in a measure while we are on this earth, but I refuse to believe that we don't have the possibility of radical healing. I have experienced it, bit by bit, and long for it for you. And that healing, well, it looks a lot like a restoration of home.

We can see this radical healing all along the way. We all have been given gifts, which speak to the sustenance he gives in the wilderness. He removes the vast desert and harsh sand to make way for a fruitful garden—even the perfection of Eden. These gifts include the people who have loved us our entire lives. Yes, they are treasures given to us who speak to the coming forever comfort of Zion.

My husband has helped me so much in the wilderness. How are you experiencing God's treasures? His presence is all around you: in the daily sunrise, in a stranger's smile, and in every act of kindness you experience. As you have heard in my story, simple things like sunlight and a listening ear can assure you that this promise is for you, too. God's desire is to bring you home and hold you; therefore, you can expect him to reach out with his measureless love through the world and people around you.

We must remember that outside of all human love is the ever-greater love of God. It's through this love that David could praise

God in the wilderness. It's through this love that Abraham could offer his only son, knowing God would provide the sacrifice. It's through this love that Elijah, on the swing of his emotions, could yet hear the "gentle whisper" of God. It's through this love that Mary could face all the uncertainty of her life and sing out of her soul a blessing to the Lord. It's through this love that Paul could say, "For to me, to live is Christ and to die is gain" (Phil. 1:21). All these found their way through the wilderness and now are a part of the "great cloud of witnesses" (Heb. 12:1), which we must let fill and renew our perspective.

And it's through this love that Jesus, in his flesh, could survive forty days in the wilderness without food or drink and still resist the great temptation of Satan to take up his deity and find life outside of the Father. He overcame through his true food, the Word of God. Can we forget all that he carried on the cross? His love must be the in and out and all around of how we see life and God. He is the only one who can make any true way for us through the wilderness.

Let us press into the truth of our homecoming right now because as our vantage point becomes clearer, we will behold the God of glory. In this beholding, we will come to be like him and will receive the strength to overcome in his name. We can learn to run again, and we will see those arms of our God reaching out to welcome us to a great homecoming just as the father welcomed his prodigal son.

For each of us, whether we have been wounded by mental illness or by so many other life-altering hardships, our God is a healer. Through him we overcome. And we overcome by coming home. When he knocks, we open the door and welcome his presence into all the moments of our lives. We say *yes* to the new day, to the radiant sky. He wants us to not only come home but to embody home, where we will receive the clarity to see his good plans for us. Because they become like the gorgeous, garden-born fruit of Eden, our true home. And we trust this plenty is the truth we need. For in the plenty is life, is home.

5

THE COLORS OF YOUR MIND
From Isolation to Intimacy

February 2015

I came home from a grueling quarrel with someone I loved and respected and simply collapsed into my husband's arms, shaking. The cutting words from a person I considered to be a dear friend sliced my mind like a sharp sword. I felt deeply wounded after this verbal assault. What had been said was dark and untrue, yet, so very, very potent.

In my mind, this person had disparaged me as a wife, mother, missionary, and child of God. I look back at this incident today, with the perspective I have gained over several years, and wonder about my friend's intentions that day. It's possible that they meant me no harm. But I had no way to consider that possibility at that time. I didn't, couldn't, realize how fragile I was, how susceptible to the undercutting of lies.

Worst of all was how my friend had claimed an inability to really know me because I presented "false faces" to others. I was accused of showing people what I wanted them to see and not my true self. Despite three years of doing life together, this friend claimed they did not—and could not—truly know me.

The accusations rocked me to the core of my existence. Would others say similar things about me? Was I truly loved or known by anyone?

I tried to remember who I really was. Loved. Redeemed. Fully accepted. Chosen. Whole. However, beginning with the words of a respected Christian friend, the lies became overpowering, drowning out the truth. The enemy, in his evil scheming, was ruthless in his attack. I was sinking down a dark hole. I scratched at its edges, nails splintered and filled with mud, but I failed to gain a grip.

As I spiraled perilously downward, I found myself in a bleak, dank, black void. Was there any way out? The air felt thin and insufficient for my hungering lungs. I gasped and fought, but to no avail. When and how would this end? I didn't know, couldn't know.

Rips in the Sky

In those days, I became a stranger to myself, spinning more and more out of control and out of touch with reality. The criticisms of my friend became a powerful tool in the hands of the enemy. I could hear the words repeated over and over again, and they left me a beaten beggar, nearly dead in the hole into which I fell.

I couldn't see ahead to bright skies. I couldn't even see a solid sky above me. The lies I heard—"You are unloved, unwanted, foolish. You are a terrible wife and mother. You have no competency in ministry"—were menacing clouds blocking the light. All the lie-hearing and identity-questioning came crashing down on me.

Soon, I would enter my full manic state and be confined in the white, cold walls of Szent Imre Kórház.

So often since then I have thought, *How did I get in such a state?* The short answer is I was living, for the most part, isolated from a safe community where I could be vulnerable. My delicate chemical balance, which was untreated, certainly played a large role. Though not altogether helpful to contemplate, I still wonder if the destructive episode could have been prevented.

I have long struggled to protect myself from damning thoughts. Growing up as a fragile, highly emotional young girl, I heard the lie that I was "too much." I also faced the lie that I was "not enough," as the "shy, awkward, ugly twin" I believed myself to be. In my early adulthood, my search for love led me to give myself away emotionally and spiritually to someone unworthy. I thought he truly loved me, but he ultimately acted selfishly, not guarding my feelings. Instead of seeing him as he truly was, I foolishly tried harder to win his love.

Weathering that early heartbreak, I found God's unconditional love in the arms of my mother. She was also a source of strength and a great comfort to me when I returned home after my first manic episode, which I will describe further in Chapter Seven. Her presence was a promise, a light along my path, pointing me to my true north. She always directed me toward Jesus and underscored the truth of how God made me uniquely to live my life with purpose.

I became unmoored when she passed from this life and I lost her voice. Most times it was just an ache I couldn't define, except to say I missed her presence in this world. So, I understand if you, too, have lost someone dear to you in any way. Their words are no longer a phone call away, and now you struggle, you feel unanchored. In Chapter Three, I shared about the importance of "naming our grief," and it is also important to acknowledge the ongoing effect of loss on our lives, our story.

In my story, just one year after my mother's death, I became a wife and eventually, a mother. And I wanted my mother then, so much. For the enemy knew my weaknesses and wasted no time in ripping apart a healthy view of myself as a mother. Instead of relishing the sweetness of caring for new life, I felt as though I just couldn't do it right. In a place deep within, I despaired.

I longed even more for my mother in those days. If I couldn't have my mother, I wanted a mom mentor to take me under her wing. But wherever I looked, I just came up empty. I felt like something was wrong with me, and I didn't know who I could talk to when days were hard.

This melancholy increasingly permeated the next seven and a half years of my inner life, from the birth of my first son in 2007 until I nearly died in a Hungarian hospital in 2015. I just wanted someone to see me, to understand how hard the loneliness and feeling like I didn't matter were.

Ironically, just a few hours before the crushing encounter with my friend, I had spent time with someone I believed could become a mom mentor to me. The hours with her had left me feeling seen and loved, just as I was. It felt like a promising step out of my isolation, yet that positive interaction could not overcome the damage of the negative words my friend spoke later that same day. I don't know how his trickery undoes us, but I know our enemy is cunning and goes right, straight to our deepest insecurity. That is demonstrated by how easily he could rip apart my sense of worth in the lie-inducing time with my once-dear friend just hours after an uplifting conversation had blessed me like a warming sun rising in my skies. However, it is clear that years of isolation are not easily overcome.

Remembering this, I understand better our fallen inheritance from the first woman to ever live. The serpent came to her and directly attacked Eve's relationship with God, which was perfect and innocent, yet naïve and fragile. He pointed his words directly toward the issue of trust. Could God really be trusted to know and offer the best for her? Had he truly placed his own indelible, eternally stunning image within her? Was he truly loving, extending himself in relationship with her, or did he just want to control her and remain superior?

We want to plead with Eve through the millennia of time and say, "Yes, trust God! He is good, and he loves you! Don't ruin this perfect world!" But how would any of us have reacted in the same situation? Would we have trusted in God's love, which seemed a bit abstract and based on potential, or taken the bright, shiny, real thing right in front of us?

In times of dark thinking, we may ask how we can be so fragile that we can let the enemy steal, destroy, and nearly kill us. I had the beautiful love of God, my husband, children, and many others. Yet, I still believed the lies over the truth.

The Devastation of Isolation

I deeply value openness and the ability to be our true selves in our relationships. Yet in those seven and a half years of deepening isolation, it was hard, so hard, to live consistently this way.

During my college and post-college years, I wrote page after page, with different bright-colored pens, to friends and family. But when I wasn't doing well, those words would dry up. They would become brittle and crack within me until they were blown away like fine dust. I now realize that most of the time we lived in Budapest, from early spring 2012 to late winter 2015, I was living in growing isolation and darkness. In those dark days, many of the words I most needed to share with others were lost within me.

Author and researcher Brené Brown says, "Vulnerability is the core, the heart, the center of meaningful human experiences."[1] If that is true, then I have lived bereft, without a core or heart of meaning for many seasons of my life. My soul weeps to think of just how desolate an existence I have allowed myself to live.

This desolation becomes so deeply attached to our truest selves. When the loneliness is present, it is hard—dust-eating hard—to mine the depths of who we truly are. We become unanchored in our human experience. The isolation can become a place, as it did with me, where our thoughts become the enemy, no matter what our personality is or how we process life.

When this isolation occurs, people can die of mental illness. We can feel so awful and alone that we are terrified to reach out, and then the darkness surges and we are gone. We are overcome.

I was almost overcome.

The darkness of my loneliness scares me and stills me, as I think about just how close I came to the point of no return. I remember the wilderness. I remember the isolation of this experience, and I have compassion with my hurting self as I think on just how difficult it can be to feel utterly alone in a dark place. Such a solitary state makes it easy to fall into a cycle of false thoughts.

Those who knew me then might find it hard to believe the desolation I felt. In the days and weeks before the darkness overwhelmed me in Budapest, I appeared to be fine. Just five days before the quarrel with my friend left me shaking and undone, I shared my story with a group of Hungarian youth on a Friday night. The tagline for my talk was, "There are a million ways to be lost, but only one way to be found." Eyes were clear and attentive as my message connected. I truly believed I had come home and had been found at last. One friend said, "The girls were looking at you and thinking, 'I want to be like her when I grow up.'" It was a high moment. Then came the cutting words from my friend. My manic episode followed soon after.

Even when I was sharing words about being lost and found, I was keeping my deepest struggles hidden. In that isolation was the reality of what remained unsettled within me. I wasn't sharing that reality—I didn't want to share it with others. I was not consciously putting on a "false face," as my former friend accused me of. But I was not experiencing the true intimacy I needed that would supply me the safety to share more of myself.

Many of us can come to this place, although it doesn't happen overnight. We start to feel things, dark things. Our thoughts spiral toward lies about our world, our God, and ourselves. Over time, we fear we are a depressing, neurotic presence to others. Then, we start omitting any descriptions of how we're *really* doing. We become experts at "fines" and "goods," not wanting to burden others with our darkness or experience their seeming pity for our problems. We are so quickly mired in the shame of our thoughts. Soon, we're slipping into the depths of isolation, and there seems to be no way out.

Here in this isolation is exactly where the enemy wants us to dwell because this mental loneliness is a potent breeding ground for the spawning of a million lies. They jam our vision with points of darkness until blindness comes. We lose our perspective; the cloud cover is so thick that we can't even make out the horizon, and we become defenseless to the onslaught.

This was true of my journey. I hated what life was doing to me. I wanted to believe I was God's beautiful one, but I felt I had messed up too many times. I longed to know the embrace of God's unconditional love, but I doubted it was real. The pressure to be all I thought I needed to be didn't give me a fighting chance at victory.

This precarious mental outlook brought me to the edge of instability. The quarrel with my friend affected me so intensely in large part because of my mental isolation. I had too few voices that could secure me in a better word spoken over me—words that would begin and end in God's perfect love. The truth and grace of the gospel were not present in those two hours, and my friend's words cut right through me.

I unraveled progressively in the next few days and weeks. As my world was caving in, I did the worst thing I could do: I retreated further into myself. I struggled to know whom I could trust. Things got worse when Jared met with my accuser while trying to mediate the conflict. But the person who had hurt me so severely twisted my words until my husband questioned whether I was speaking the truth.

It was hideous how the enemy wove himself about the inner workings of those unraveling days. I lost the ability to trust my husband to understand what was really happening. This distrust was crucial to the evil one's plan to destroy my life. Soon, I felt defenseless as the delusions and visions—all of an intense spiritual nature—began.

When isolation turned me inward, it was only a matter of time before the full manifestation of my undiagnosed bipolar disorder would lay itself bare. I barely left my bedroom. I barely ate. I barely saw my precious husband or children. I didn't sleep at all. I was almost totally isolated.

In this cut-off state, my very life was soon hanging in the balance as I became unmoored, isolated from others and, really, from myself.

The Mending Begins

I believe in wholeness, both for myself and for you. I offer my testimony to help convince you that you can also experience healing. What is torn apart can be mended. There is a redeemed perspective that can make you whole.

Those lies I nearly believed about myself in those dark days before admittance to the hospital in Budapest seem so foreign to me now. I have seen the kindness of God make me great. He has given me new relationships and a beautiful vista of community to replace the desert days of loneliness that obscured my view. He has given me people to help sew my world back together. And more than that, he has given me himself, in truer and more glorious ways than I could have ever imagined.

Even before I left the hospital in Hungary, God brought Izzy. We were born the same year, 1974, a mere month apart. She was a writer, too, and a part of our ministry to Hungarian students. Although we had met a few years earlier, our friendship still felt new. As she came to the hospital each day, our souls knit together. It was so beautiful how she looked at me as though I were normal and sane and treated me as if I were highly valued and worth knowing. She was an angel to me in those days.

Then there was my twin, Sara, who took hold of my hand as I lay on my bed in our Budapest flat after returning from the hospital. Everything was still so fresh. I couldn't sleep much at all. I was frayed mentally with the onslaught of delusions and the accompanying visions of cataclysmic battles. It felt like I had become a part of the battle scenes in my dark days, and it seemed like I was fighting for my life in every way. I was so tired, so very tired.

As Sara held my hand, I thanked God for this twin sister who had been with me even when we were first formed in our mother's womb. The tenacity she had shown to come thousands of miles to be with me was soul-healing. She spoke a gem of truth, declaring, "God is going to bring you through this so fully, Abby."

Another sister, Kristen, also came to Budapest after I returned from the hospital, rearranging her demanding life to be present with me. We took walks daily around the neighborhood and stopped at the coffee shop across the street from our flat. We talked as sisters and friends. When she looked at me, she did not see a deranged woman but someone who was whole. I dreamed with her about the future and began to believe I would have one.

As we returned to the States, I continued to battle to sleep and know true rest for my mind. Yet, day by day, I grew stronger, fed by the love of my husband's family, who lived very close to the missionary house where we stayed. One day, as we did often, I was chatting with my mother-in-law in her kitchen while she made dinner, when she spontaneously proclaimed, "Oh Abby, I am so glad you are better!" That proclamation bloomed as love between us, rooted in a fresh sense of what we had built over the thirteen years she had been in my life.

Little words. Small sentences. Time spent in regular things. It all served to remind me that love was real and meant for me— even now. I had not messed up so much that I had driven away the love of God and others. On the contrary, each relationship felt more precious, each conversation mending my torn vision by another stitch or two, allowing me to glimpse a radiance unknown in previous days.

Then there was God.

I was so frail. After we returned from Hungary, side effects of the medicine I took to calm my bipolar disorder hindered even my ability to walk. I would shuffle up the hill of the cemetery by the mission house with an altered gait of small, unsure steps, listening to "My Lighthouse" by Rend Collective.[2] I began to believe my legs would dance again as my mind did when I listened to this song. I took just one little step at a time, believing again God wanted me and loved me.

None of it was easy. But I learned to treasure the days. I learned to look for the truth, knowing anew how sacred it was. I clung to the words of those who loved me as they fought for my return to life. I began to cling, moment by moment, to the deepest, purest reality of the love of God. It felt like I was a tiny, helpless baby sometimes. Yet, as a babe, I could rest in the affection of God because he is the author of beauty from ashes, new life from death.

With each breath, it seemed as though my intimacy with God became more robust, and my sky was brightening one sunbeam at a time. Our relationship was a living thing, which felt tied to each heartbeat, each healing touch that I needed to live again. Worship songs flew from the screen at church or from my phone to a song I could sing whole-heartedly. His love was real, and I would forever know it.

Albeit cautiously, I also began to trust God for deepening relationships with others who were new to me. I felt insecure, especially when I returned to church, just a little over a week after we came home from Hungary. I had been prayed for by many in this supporting church while I had been hospitalized. While

I was thankful for those prayers, knowing that this church knew details of my hospital stay made me feel exposed, and I worried that these people would view me only in the light of my struggle. But the Lord would bring a sweet word to help me know I was seen, ultimately, by him. This happened the first week, when a friend approached me after the service and said, "You are very brave to be here." It was so good to have someone affirm that simply showing up took courage during this very early stage of healing. She sealed this affirmation with a warm embrace.

I also received a gift in a dear friendship with another fellow writer, Michelle. We had met once at a bloggers' conference, and now we began to send audio messages back and forth. They made me feel so human, so worthy of being known. She asked straightforward questions about what I had been through, never making me feel threatened by her probing—only pursued and loved. In return, she shared her own journey, making herself vulnerable as well. I received this gift as a symbol of what true and good friendship could be.

In each of these relationships, God brought greater understanding of intimacy with him and others, altering the perspective I had of myself, the world, and God. Through these dear ones' commitment to God and his love, I discovered the roots of my hope that he could buy back what I had lost. I grew up in stature, as someone I could call worthy of knowing. A fresh intimacy with God and others rose from the ashes of all that the lies had destroyed.

Woven into the Skies

Our relationships are held in a tension between those we love and share life with on one hand and the God who undergirds all our love and truth on the other. We are constantly learning, in all our various personalities of introvert or extrovert, how to maintain a healthy tension between these two. Even if we want to, we can't replace one with the other.

As we pursue intimacy, we must learn to live in the tension of balancing true connection with both God and others. If we don't, all our relationships become shallow and inauthentic. We cannot bind the truth of who we are solely to the words of love and affirmation of others, and we cannot bind this same truth solely to the love and affirmation of God. We need both. Because our understanding, our laying hold of the truth and the love of God, is manifest through genuine relationship with God *and* with others.

As I shared earlier, we moved from Pennsylvania to Florida five months after returning from Hungary. As I navigated new relationships in a very closely confined community, I felt this tension acutely. I wanted to pull inward and just lean on God, cutting others out. After all, wasn't God the only one who could love me perfectly?

Yes, this is true. But none of us can really experience all the benefits of God's love without the human experience of relationship. As we trust others, we hear God speak to us through them. Their love and acceptance, whether they know our story or not, reveals to us that God is making us whole.

In May of 2016, after nine months of deep, life-giving community, I suffered another breakdown that required a return to a mental ward, this time in Orlando. My husband, therapist, and I struggled to understand what prompted this breakdown and agreed that it could have been triggered in part because I was contemplating leaving behind the beautiful people I had grown close to during this community-based internship. It was so different than the isolated environment where I had been living before my breakdown in Hungary, and I didn't want to leave it.

This same community also made the fallout from my manic episode feel so different than my episode in Hungary. In Florida, I was surrounded by those who knew me and expressed their love for me just as I was. I was anchored by intimacy with others, which was vital because the understanding of my relationship with God became skewed and untrustworthy at the height of my manic times.

The day I was released from University Behavioral Center happened to be my birthday. I chose to go to a Disney World park and was met there by my family and my friends. Because I was not yet stable, it was a strange, yet beautiful, day. I was glad to see that my children had missed me but had not been traumatized by my hospitalization. And I knew that my friends had come to Disney that day for me. I saw love everywhere I looked, and it was a beautiful experience.

The next few days brought some of the darkest of my mental illness, but I continued to be surrounded by people who loved me, as I truly was. I felt seen and known. They made me feel as though I was only temporarily and incompletely affected by mental illness. In their eyes, I really was the one they knew as friend and beloved sister in Christ.

And in this fertile ground, new life, fledgling yet strong, sprang forth. I was reassured that God loved me still because those around me showed me this ripe fruit, this choice love. Therefore, though I was not fully well, the friendships I knew in those days created power to comprehend "the breadth and length and height and depth" of the love of Christ (Eph. 3:18 ESV). This intimate community gave me courage as I moved forward with my life. I wasn't isolated in the lies of the enemy. I could stand in the truth of God.

I want to be clear here: our relationship with God is the most important one in our lives. But there is a fullness to that relationship that comes through community and further inspires our intimacy with him and others. This synergy brings the Spirit of God to life as he is manifested through the presence of others. We know his kindness, intentional care, and abiding love in ways we could not without tangible expressions through community.

As I came through to the other side of my second hospitalization, I felt a boldness in my relationship with God that I had never known before. He was mending the wounds in my heart and using so many beautiful people to do so.

I took up the strength of others who stood in the gap between the building of my stability and its experiential reality in my life. I regained my will to fight the long battle yet before me. Because of their love, I remembered it was worth the effort to overcome the isolation that had nearly killed me in Budapest. This love was most profoundly seen through the heart of my husband—his patience and continual love most exemplified in acts of service for me and our children.

Because I had been so entrenched in lies, this move from isolation to intimacy was not an easy process. But I learned that in those deep-down, shredded places of my soul, the image of God within me remained intact. And his image in me caused me to long for the fullest possible relationship with him.

In the early days after leaving Hungary and then after my relapse in Orlando, my journey toward stability and wholeness looked like one hard-fought stitch at a time. It involved a lot of anguished questioning while resting in love at the same time. It took a lot of calls and texts to friends and family made with a stubborn intent to remain in relationship. This pursuit of intimacy with God and others was how I fought for true life—the one I wanted.

And this good God kept giving. Amid each one of my doubts and the vast wasteland of my sense of failure, he gave me more of himself. His was a tender love that made and upheld the true vision of my life. The faintest touch of his healing hand could solidify the identity I had in his indestructible love. Each day produced a greater passion to live in deepening intimacy with God and others.

And in this true living, I committed to reach out in community to share my story. I choose to share to bring you close, friend. And I choose to speak loudly and clearly the truth that you, too, can overcome. You, too, can and will gaze firmly upon that priceless, glorious, inexhaustible sunrise that is becoming the reality of your life.

6

BRIGHTER DAYS COMING
From Shame to Freedom

March 2015

I sat on an old wooden chair as the nurse prodded and poked my hand, looking for a vein to draw yet more blood. So many vials of blood had been drawn during my time at Szent Imre Kórház that no more veins were available in my arms. I never learned why they needed so much of my blood, but I was ashamed that my arms were covered in prick marks. I thought they looked like the arms of a drug addict.

The blood draws were just part of the shame-ridden experiences that stripped me of my dignity in the Hungarian hospital. There were those circulation-stopping straps binding my ankles and wrists to that corner hospital bed. There was the flimsy, cloth gown that didn't sufficiently cover me. There was the diaper I was wearing when I awoke in the ICU. All proved that I was helpless and at the mercy of those who cared for me.

The shame seeped into my body in all possible ways—physically, emotionally, spiritually, and mentally—as I became more aware of life. There was no escaping it.

The Cloaking and Soaking

Szent Imre Kórház in Budapest, Hungary, and University Behavioral Center (UBC) in Orlando, Florida, are worlds apart, geographically and in other ways. In Budapest, they tried to restrain and sedate me out of my alternate reality. At UBC, they took a more hands-off approach.

In both locations, I felt I was being treated like a child—or like someone who was only her chemical makeup. Like my mental state was the beginning and end of my story. There was enough of me present to comprehend what people around me thought about me. The shame of it all made me desperate to leave the care facilities. In Szent Imre Kórház, I went to the window twice to escape. I tried to leave UBC within the first couple of days, but I didn't make it past the first employee in the cafeteria.

The day after I was admitted to UBC, I began banging my head repeatedly against a concrete wall. I was hearing a "voice," the exact sound of someone I knew, commanding me to smash my head so I could experience the tiniest bit of the apocalyptic pain I was causing the whole world.

As they took me by ambulance to the hospital, this voice continued to speak in awful ways about how I had destroyed the cosmos. In the height of both manic-driven states, I was "told" that I was a type of "queen of evil" who had destroyed every beautiful thing. I had been complicit to the acts of evil worked throughout time, and even, somehow, contributed to them. It sounds wildly outlandish to write it out, but in those times, there was nothing more real, and that prompts its own kind of shame.

When I looked at my release papers from UBC, I was shocked to discover a new diagnosis of "schizophrenia," a type of psychosis often characterized by consistent voices, escalating delusions, and a state of confusion, and notes that I had been admitted under the "Baker Act," which meant I had been admitted against my will.[1] My therapist disagreed with UBC's diagnosis, saying at worst I suffered from detachment from reality related to my bipolar symptoms. My husband disagreed with the Baker Act statement, saying I had admitted myself willingly. But I wasn't sure what I believed—I remember many strange things happening when I first entered UBC—and at the end of this shameful experience, the dark clouds on those papers revealed how the professionals viewed my skies.

Although these two institutions were the safest locations for me at the time of my manic episodes, the trauma of my treatment wrapped a good deal of shame around me. Even more shame-inducing were the damning false narratives I was hearing in my head from the enemy of truth. Everywhere I looked, I was covered in inescapable shame.

Existence had ceased to be under my control. I was merely a soul bereft of self. In all the pain, I had all but lost my humanity. As Bessel van der Kolk writes, "trauma robs you of the feeling that you are in charge of yourself."[2] That's exactly how I felt. And I wondered how I would ever regain any sense of control in my life. Neither my mind nor my body were my own, and anger and shame were my constant companions. It was all overwhelming.

As I began to walk the road of recovery, it became clear that these wounds of shame were interspersed in my deepest heart places. Because they seemed to grow in darkness like a black, inky river, I found it difficult to believe I could truly be healed. Van der Kolk puts it well: "The challenge of recovery is to reestablish ownership of your body and your mind or your self. This means feeling free to know what you know and feel what you feel without becoming overwhelmed, enraged, ashamed or collapsed."[3]

Because shame and fear are linked in their long-ago spawning, fear has entrenched itself with that shame, and both emotions try to convince me that I will have to go back into the hospital, that I will lose my dignity and sense of self, yet again. Shame can be relentless.

The truth is, I cannot say with certainty that I will never have to return to the hospital. Yet I must push past the messages of shame and fear to receive the certainty of my faith. I must direct myself toward the truth that in all things I can overcome through the reality of God's goodness and faithfulness.

Friend, you must also pursue full healing from the steeping of shame that occurs in our trauma. We must all learn to trust the God of wholeness to bring us to completion, and we must turn away from any shortcuts to healing for they are merely bandages that cannot cleanse our open wounds.

Although it may be odd to say, we can thank shame for the freedom God has brought and continues to bring into our lives. If we had not been wounded so deeply by shame, we wouldn't need the healing. If this wounding had not taken nearly everything from us, we might be able to settle for false forms of healing, such as success, beauty, affirmation from others, or simply distraction from the pain.

Willing to be honest about the depth of our pain and the depth of our shame is crucial to healing. Van der Kolk describes this process as authentic living and says, "As long as you keep secrets and suppress information, you are fundamentally at war with yourself. . . . The critical issue is allowing yourself to know what you know. That takes an enormous amount of courage."[4] Offering my story to you is an exercise in courage. I intend for it to be deeply placed encouragement that will help you to find a way to know and own your story, too.

Shame can no longer be a passive thing, trapped in a million layers and sinews of our bodies. If we want to know ourselves and live in freedom, we have to acknowledge the trauma we have endured and how much it has affected our stories. There will be no life if we do not have the courage to face the devastating experiences that cause pain in our bodies. For the sake of our full mental health and the peace of all whose stories are tied to ours, we must walk this road of courage.

Because the striking reality of shame finds us, we are roused within to strike back at it. The lies of our mental illness stain the holiest places of our spirituality. There is no way to life without dealing with the grotesque reality of our innermost shame.

The simplest answer to the problem of our shame is "Immanuel, God with us" (Matt. 1:23). The God who took on the flesh of humanity and all the shame ever known is the only true, triumphant answer to it. We begin to cling fiercely to the treasure of how God, in the form of Jesus, comes to be with us amid all the brokenness of this world. Therefore, we can know he is present in our deepest shame.

Everyday Occurrences

We need the courage to face our pain not only when we look at our most traumatic moments but also when we face the mundane of every day. While there is a grueling reality to the traumatic and shameful loss of dignity in many of our journeys, everyday shame can be even harder to uncover and understand.

It's the kind of shame you feel in a "normal" conversation when you discover you are drooling because of the side effects of your medicine. It's the shame that comes when your mental illness surfaces for the first time in a conversation with a fairly new friend. It's the shame you feel when others just don't know what to say when you share a part of your story, and so they nervously share about someone they know who has a mental illness, too. It's a world of beautiful people not knowing how to deal with something that is so often hidden or discussed in hushed and—yes—ashamed, tones.

Mental illness is a part of humanity's struggle this side of Eden. An estimated 26 percent of Americans ages eighteen and older—about one in four adults—suffer from a diagnosable mental disorder in a given year.[5] With the recent stresses added by the COVID-19 pandemic, the number of people diagnosed with some form of mental illness has increased significantly, with rates of severe anxiety and depression jumping over 20 percent in 2021 compared with 2019.[6] As the rates of infection rise and fall, the long-term implications of the crisis on mental health are unknown.

God never intended mental illness for his perfect world, so we must collectively work to overcome it in the light of God's love. A big part of overcoming mental illness is eradicating the shame surrounding it. As mental illness can be hereditary, generations of families are sometimes plagued with the silent shame of it all.[7]

For me, overcoming the daily occurrences of shame has meant clinging hard to truth when a careless word has the potential to further cloud my skies. It is standing tall, clothed in my identity as God's beloved, and refusing to bow to the cunning, surprisingly powerful allure of shame. We can be drawn toward shame because sometimes we just want to hide in our wounds. And nothing keeps them more hidden than shame.

Ironically, bowing to shame can cause more shame—making us feel ashamed that we are not strong enough to overcome our shame. The only true solution is to, once again, face what lies within. Brené Brown, an influential researcher on shame, notes that "if we don't come to terms with our shame, our struggles, we start believing that there's something wrong with us—that we're bad, flawed, not good enough—even worse we start acting on those beliefs."[8]

Refusing to deal with our shame empowers the inner tyrant who fights relentlessly against the healing we so crave. Shame can so overtake our inner world that we clam up and refuse to share ourselves. Shame presses us down, separating us from our glorious potential. We use humor, defensiveness, or any number of tactics, some very harmful, to avoid being vulnerable. But our actions prevent us from bringing our shame into the healing light of the love of God, the one we can trust to never, ever leave us and to always support us.

The trauma of my shame forced me to mine the depths of my inner, spiritual narrative. My mental weakness in the times of severe mania led to lie-infused inner voices that told me, "You are unworthy to exist." "You are unlovable." The lies were squarely opposed to the truth of God's love; but in those dark times, the lies felt so real.

The everyday reality of my shame forced me to deal relationally with it and with the depth of my mania-induced self-hatred.

It has been healing to show up in the presence of others—whether in my writing or in face-to-face dialogue. It has been necessary to prove the truth to myself again and again: I am loved. Therefore, I can be open and honest about my struggles, no matter what response I get.

For me—as for all who deal with deep levels of shame—I can hit walls that make me want to run and hide even as I exercise my courage. But if we persist and push through the wall, we will find something truer, more beautiful, is waiting: a resilience able to face even the most shame-laced experiences. Instead of burying our shame, we lift up a beautiful vulnerability that rewrites the story we are telling.

It was while I was unable to even walk properly due to side effects from my medication that I first heard God say, "I want you to share your story—the one you're living now." I was terrified. How could I reveal what seemed like my greatest shame to the world?

When I wrote my first blog post about my journey with bipolar disorder, I sat for a long time, scared to hit "publish." I didn't necessarily feel better when I did, but I knew I had been obedient to God's calling to share my story, and there was great peace in that.

To be an overcomer in mental illness requires us to be aware that our journey will be lifelong. While healing is real and great victories are possible, we must stay in the fight and consistently battle our shame. I have been humbled when I realize that I have missed an opportunity to share my story with a perfectly safe person because I was hiding behind my wall of shame. I must remember the need to be vulnerable. And I must acknowledge that the battle against shame will not leave me for even one day before that long and beautiful embrace of heaven.

Taking a Stand

I've shared a lot already about what it has looked like to stand tall in the story of my life, showing up wholeheartedly. Brené Brown writes that "the Wholehearted identify vulnerability as the catalyst for courage, compassion, and connection."[9] Since shame is a shared part of our inheritance, we take a stand, not only for ourselves, but also for others when we share our story in a vulnerable way. I believe we can all make ourselves more vulnerable, and I humbly hope to inspire you to boldly share your own story. To say out loud those things that shame you most.

Most of us can show up by speaking light into the generations—those who have come before us and those who are yet to come. Mental illness runs all through my family lines, so I share my story to honor the active silence of my past. I hold sacred those whose endurance and fight only occasionally overcame their illness in this life. I also convey the truth of who I am, what my life has encompassed. I speak clearly about being on the path toward overcoming for those who will come behind me.

There is still much work to do, I realize. Recently, when I had the chance to share my story, I felt ashamed when I heard others describe my journey as "tragedy," "heavy," and "hard." It wasn't meant to be a shame-inducing environment, and in fact, it was a very safe environment where we shared our stories collectively. But the shame I felt was real. Especially as I thought of the burden of carrying the shame of loved ones who came before me and what has befallen me in my life and what may come in the years ahead in the lives of my children.

However, I have come to realize that although I can't control whether my children will battle mental illness at some point in their lives, I can live in a way that will ensure the shame of mental illness doesn't stick to them. They will see that I do not allow mental illness to hover like a dark cloud in my life—at least not every day. They will see me live courageously and wholeheartedly, confronting the lethal possibilities of shame by saying, "No More!" I will do this in my life and, through me, in the lives of those I love. I will lift up a radiant vision with every shade of promise.

I can work toward this goal by offering tender words to build up my children in their shame-inducing moments. When stern words could cause them to hide, I will call them with a gentle, clear voice into the grace and love of God. With this, I extend full forgiveness for their wrong. And when they have done nothing wrong, I can teach them again about the fallen effects of shame and how we stand with Jesus and his redemption to say again, "No more!"

When we stand tall together, we can see the culture change. As I have shared my story, I have been encouraged to hear others' stories in return. At times, their stories have caused me to rise in courage, and I am deeply thankful for how community brings strength to us all.

Shame cannot stand when we tower over it as redeemed humanity. We are not made to see only the vision of our own sky—the fabric of our personal story. Rather, we are made to view our lives as pieces of a heavenly quilt, with each beautiful, messy, glorious piece bringing uniqueness and definition. As my sky touches yours, I share with you the beauty of what I have come to see.

I offer the words in this book as my humble gift and audaciously believe they can help clear your own sky as you connect to the great mender: God and his Holy Spirit. And as you rise up to share your story, the unique beauty of your sky will touch my own.

The National Weather Service discovered a few years ago how skies over one part of the world can affect the skies many thousands of miles away when it began tracking how the jet stream affected the Sahara Desert. With satellite imagery and careful monitoring, it began to notice how dust storms in the Sahara travel around the world and can affect many parts of the United States and other far-flung countries. One gorgeous effect is the deepening of the colors of the sunset. Our own time-and-space sunset sky can be even more stunning because another sky has touched ours. This, my friend, is precisely how our stories can impact the living, breathing glory of another's story and enhance the beauty of their sky.

Most of all, we see the eternal perfect sky of God changing ours, rewriting our stories and changing our perspectives. The Spirit of God brings healing that reaches to the root of our shame. Providing the sweet balm of Gilead, bringing together what has been ripped apart, making things altogether new. Full healing finds itself through none other than God.

Psalm 34:5 says, "Those who look to him are radiant, and their faces shall never be ashamed" (ESV). I meditated upon this passage before I went into the hospital in Hungary; and in the days during and after my hospital stay, I saw it for the promise it was.

For all of us, the declaration of our radiance can shake off shame's deepest covering. This happens as we gaze upon the face of the gracious, loving God who calls us to lock eyes with him.

It is simple, poignant, and profound—as we gaze upon God, we are transformed. A. W. Tozer writes, "Faith is the gaze of a soul upon a saving God."[10] This is what faith is: looking to, gazing upon God, the one who has saved us, once and for all time. When our gaze is upon him, his own eyes will never cease to meet ours. And those eyes will be full of the love of the ages, building us up in all this goodness. This is how we become strong and steady. This is how we are uplifted until we can't help but stand.

My dream is for a revolution, or renewal, of such living. I would love to see you, friend, stand in the goodness and grace of God, meeting that bully, shame, as it tries to tear down your beautiful vision of God. I would love for you to stand and, with your striking radiance, defeat shame in your life!

This is the beauty of a million skies or a million ways our vision can be cast toward our lives. Yes, there are many dark skies, stormy and foreboding, which our trials can lead us to see. There are also the ripped and torn skies revealing what appear to be black voids in distant, starless space. Here, all seems lost. But beyond and within every sky is the sovereign presence of God. He, Jesus, "upholds the universe by the word of his power" (Heb. 1:3 ESV). Essentially, effortlessly, Jesus holds it all. He is our truest and eternal vision, and he will never fail us. Beyond the rips and tears inflicted by shame, with its clinging darkness, is the sunshine of God, ever ready to make you radiant—beyond the power of any shame.

What Freedom Looks Like

What does life look like on the other side of shame? Can you imagine? Can you dream of your face in a constant state of radiance as you receive into your soul, through faith, all that God is? Friend, how can the cloak of shame continue to cover you?

Is it hard to imagine a life of such freedom when you are used to carrying that sense of being "less than," which so often comes with mental illness or other inner struggles? If your answer is yes, I want you to know that I am right with you. I am good at being vulnerable enough to talk about what shame looks like in my life. I am good at casting a vision of a different reality. I am good at offering a call to action. But pushing through to the reality of God's freedom and consistently living in that reality? This is my struggle.

I don't want to beat myself up or discourage you. I have already spoken about being vulnerable, sharing our stories, and standing tall against shame as we embrace God's glorious vision for our lives. This posture is essential to obtaining the kind of freedom we crave. But we are not meant to experience only a momentary triumph or even a dramatic, singular experience. We are meant to possess what Jesus desires for us when he says, "I have come that they may have life, and have it to the full" (John 10:10). Nothing less than this full life is his will.

However, for many of us, Jesus's vision seems impossible. We ask how living such a life would be possible. Paul, in Colossians 2:6 answers, "So then, just as you received Christ Jesus as Lord, continue to live your lives in him." In faith, we see ourselves in God's arms fully accepted, because Jesus died to bring us to God. We live breath by breath this way until we are forever in the presence of God. As we look to God and experience his power, strength, and love, things like shame cannot chain us. We are free.

For me, this looks a lot like a mental boxing match. I win. But my face is a bit bloody and bruised.

I am completely in love with the song "This Is Me"[11] from the movie *The Greatest Showman*.[12] Repeatedly, the lyrics assert, "I am brave. I am bruised. I am who I'm meant to be. This is me."

In the movie, as this song is performed, the "misfits" come walking through the crowd of the refined. They have been shamed their entire lives for who they are. Nevertheless, they walk out strong, standing tall, heads held high, singing, "This is me." They are exhibiting a gorgeous picture of the freedom from shame God wants for us. Because the love, salvation, and full acceptance of God brings a perfect freedom, we can walk stronger and taller than the misfits in the movie.

I also love the song "Scars," by I Am They, which illustrates how God can make a beautiful testimony from our wounds, our scars.[13] In the first verse there is a phrase, "and these wounds are a story You'll use." The song continues with the chorus, "so I'm thankful for the scars, 'cause without them I wouldn't know Your heart. And I know they'll always tell of who You are."

The shame created by each of those wounds can become our greatest beauty because in the hands of God, the wounds are shaping the inner places of our hearts. Through God's healing, we can exhibit a resilience that makes us unstoppable. We find courage to stand under any dark sky, knowing our well-being is in God's hands and his light will overcome any darkness.

Can you imagine all of us awake to the light and standing strong in the full love of God? This world would look strikingly different if we could so embrace the love of God given fully in Jesus. Accepting this love, which sees us, knows all about us, and embraces us completely, can heal the brokenness. It would be the full reflection of that light that cannot be overcome. How beautifully 2 Corinthians 3:18 would come to life: "And we all, with unveiled face, beholding the glory of the Lord, are being transformed into the same image from one degree of glory to another" (ESV). There would be such exquisite glory, which could never, ever be contained.

I am going to risk my heart here and say I dare to believe this is possible. But if it is to happen, we must all release our shame. You, friend, need to believe, in this moment, as you read these words, that healing is for you—the kind of healing that means the darkness can no longer touch you, as it has before.

Begin to experience now the embrace you will know forever. We are made for eternal relationship with God. And his desire for that relationship with us causes him to reach out in love to us, continually. With this partnership we obtain freedom to live as the human race was originally created to live. In the end, as we wander in the wilderness of our exile, we all live as prodigals, running away from or simply resisting the full embrace of God's welcoming, comforting love. We wear our shame as a shield because we are so afraid his arms are not real or truly powerful enough. But they are!

Our turning away is a part of the gutting-it-out kind of pain we endure while we wait for our faith to be turned to sight. But more potent than our shame or our pain is the longing to be united with the one for whom we are made. He is all we truly want and he is ours, the ultimate freedom from our shame—that gorgeous sky of our true, unhindered beholding.

7

CRIMSON COVERS THE DARKNESS
From Fear to Love

My return to the mental ward from the Hungarian ICU gave me hope that I had endured the ugliest part of this trial. Yet, sleep still eluded me. When I closed my eyes, visions returned of angels and demons and wars in the celestial realms. My mind had not yet fully returned to me, and I didn't know when it would.

My breath felt shallow. It caught on the fear of all that remained to haunt me. Then the beating drum in my mind and heart began, and the war raged on. I felt the night convulsing like some ravaged animal. I knew I couldn't keep going like this. I had to find a way to sleep, to discover a calm beyond the terror.

Just five weeks prior, after we had returned from a conference in the Middle East, I had collapsed on my bed and slept for ten hours straight. The conference had been exhausting, and the kids had all shared a room with Jared and me. So when they were finally sleeping at home, it was our turn. And I had enjoyed the gift of the weary—sweet sleep.

How could I change so much in just a handful of weeks? I thought back longingly to that night of ten glorious hours of restful sleep. In my current state, I couldn't imagine it ever happening again. Like a torturous Tilt-A-Whirl, my mind went around and around.

And always present: the fear.

I had to find a way through. Those first nights out of the ICU, I got ready for bed at about eight, after dinner and Jared's sweet daily visit, wishing I were anywhere but this hospital. I put in my iPod earbuds and listened over and over to "Endless Hallelujah," my heart resonating each time with these lines: "We will worship, worship You / And endless hallelujah to the King."[1]

I loved how saturated these lines were with the promise of forever in God's presence. If my mind was going to be stuck, I wanted it to be stuck on something like this.

In those days, I knew so little about who I was and what would happen next for me and my family, although it had become clear that we needed to return to the States and leave the life in Hungary that we had worked so hard to obtain.

I didn't just *feel* fear—my worst fears were coming to life. Fear of failure. Fear of disappointing others or being disappointed by them. Fear of being called crazy or even unstable. Fear of being misunderstood. Fear of messing things up for Jared, who loved our current ministry. Fear of hurting my family, causing them pain, strain, and heavy worry. Fear of being so heavily medicated that I'd cease to be myself.

It was all too much. I couldn't handle this load of fear. And I definitely couldn't carry it through my sleepless nights.

When You're Rescued from the Pit

My words in this book have been strong and confident because of God and his Word. No moment in my journey has caused me to doubt that the Word became flesh and dwelled among us as the perfect Son of God. Yet all of God and his Word has been tested by the raging and at times hurricane-force winds of my continued struggle with bipolar disorder. I had fought hard during my hospital stay, pressing into his love. However, my battle with the stark darkness of fear was far from over.

The nights of little sleep continued as we left Hungary and made our way across the ocean to our physical refuge of home and community support in Souderton, Pennsylvania. As I shared in Chapter Three, we had been given the entire mission house at one of our supporting churches. It was a true grace, a shelter amid the storm.

For the first week, my daughter, then a blonde cherub of five, would come into my bedroom in the middle of every night and ask the same thing each time: "Mommy, I just wanted to ask—Are you having a good sleep?" Although I was rarely asleep, I would answer, "Yes, honey." She would go back to bed and not remember any of it in the morning. This unusual yet tender recurrence served as the sweetest affirmation from God that he was with me and those I loved most.

As time went on, my body began to respond to the sleep medication, and I began to get close to six hours of sleep a night. But I knew the medication was habit-forming, so I tried to wean myself off it a few months later, after we had moved to Orlando. Doing that and lowering the dosage of one of my other medications caused me to spiral back into sleeplessness and full-out mania, and I wound up in the hospital again.

As I recovered from that episode, I wondered deeply if the crimson shade of Jesus's sacrificial love was even meant for me. The battle was so fierce because I had seen many personally damning storm-tossed visions during this time of insomnia. How would I survive a second mental wrecking so soon? Oh, the raging fear—it was with me again.

One of my darkest episodes came after I left the Orlando hospital. After my hospitalization in Hungary, we had been able to apply for medical leave, which gave me much-needed space and time to put myself back together in some way. But I did not get enough recovery time in Orlando due to the requirements of our internship and my lack of understanding about how frail I remained. One particular night I was plagued by horrific, evil thoughts, and they were all I could hear. It marked the darkest void I had ever experienced. One voice, which appeared as Lucifer in my delusions, told me I would kill myself that night. I lay in bed, shivering, unable to move. The unthinkable seemed but a few steps away.

All signs of the blood-bought love that casts out all fear had disappeared. Lucifer hissed that Jesus as the true Son of God never existed. And even if Jesus did exist, according to the evil voice, I had corrupted myself with so much darkness that God no longer wanted me. It was a dank, mildewed, slimy pit I was in. No light shone from above. The stars and moon hid themselves. All I could perceive was the immense void.

I survived. But only because of divine hands holding me and dear ones praying for me. Their intercession allowed me to endure the black night of fear. The image of God within me could not be destroyed. At that time, I didn't understand I would be brought forever into the presence of God by my unbreakable bond with Jesus and the power of the Spirit.

My fear did not disappear in the light of day. It continued to surround me with shadows and hateful words: *God is done with you. You're not—nor were you ever—his.* The delusions raged on in a living hell I longed desperately to leave.

As he has done throughout my journey, God at that time used the words and prayers of others to stand in the places I couldn't. However, this relapse into intense mania was different than my days in the ICU in Hungary, when the thousand and more prayed me to life and continued to pray for me. Now it was only a few, who God seemed to give to me in order to see me through.

As Aaron and Hur had supported Moses in the Israelites' battle against Amalek, I was uplifted by Keda and another woman, Sufen, who were both mighty in prayer. They were vital in my victory against certain onslaughts of darkness. One afternoon, I was experiencing what I believe to have been a demonic attack. I texted both Keda and Sufen. The attack lifted within minutes.

Keda later encouraged me, describing God looking at me as his warrior daughter. Her words spoke deeply of a love that wouldn't let me go. A few weeks later, she wrote to tell me how God had shown her that Jared and I had attained victory in all we had been through. I received that word, and it reflected God's love in a way I had not been allowing myself to embrace. Through her words, I could again walk toward God, who was calling me to the sunshine of his love.

On another night shortly after my Orlando hospital stay, when I was afraid of the night's terror, I heard my daddy pray for me as he had so many times before. He prayed from Psalm 91, acknowledging that I was under God's "pinions" (wings)

(Ps. 91:4 ESV). And then he prayed something I'll never forget: "You own her, and you own her forever." In the Spirit, he knew I needed to hear that God held me from before time and into eternity. My father's words echo Jesus's words to his, and my, Heavenly Father: "My Father, who has given them to me, is greater than all; no one can snatch them out of my Father's hand" (John 10:29). It was a loosening of the enemy's strangling attempts to convince me I had sinned too greatly and lost God's love forever.

Believing in our Savior is everything to the heart of a Christ follower. But when the mind has been compromised, a person needs to be lifted on eagles' wings—the prayers and devotion of others—to move forward in the love of God. In his goodness, he seeks us and finds us through the collective strength of his people.

Perfect Love—Our Refuge

In all the blackness of my fear, I knew the blood-bought love of my Savior could move me to a place of incredible warmth and forever acceptance.

Depending on where you stand spiritually, you might not think it's a stroke of brilliance to consult the Bible in times of fear. Maybe you don't believe it will help. Or maybe you believe it should help, but you don't know how to apply the truth of God's Word to your difficult struggle. So you feel lost when you hear someone tell you to "claim the Word" or "get into Scripture," as if they are practically banging your shattered mind with the Bible.

Oh, friend, no. God's Word is meant to be a foundation, a refuge. It's meant to be warm, loving arms wrapped around us in our times of need. It's meant to still the terror, to come like a mother eagle and carry us out of the hell of our kingdom of fears.

Long before I landed in the mental ward of a Hungarian hospital, I began to memorize and meditate on Scripture. All my life, the Bible has been a blessing—leading, guiding, and grounding me. When I became a mom, I found that meditating on Bible passages fed me because I could recall those words at any time—while nursing my baby, racing toy cars across the porch with my son, or cooking dinner.

Just before that first hospital stay, I had been knee deep in 1 John 4:14–18. I had fully memorized it and recalled it again and again as I fought my way past fear. As I meditated on the passage, I experienced what often occurs when we dwell on any passage of Scripture: it was giving me new life, cleaning my windshield, so I could see the truth of a sunny day.

> And we have seen and testify that the Father has sent his Son to be the Savior of the world. Whoever confesses that Jesus is the Son of God, God abides in him, and he in God. So we have come to know and to believe the love that God has for us. God is love, and whoever abides in love abides in God, and God abides in him. By this is love perfected with us, so that we may have confidence for the day of judgment, because as he is so also are we in this world. There is no fear in love, but perfect love casts out fear. For fear has to do with punishment, and whoever fears has not been perfected in love. (ESV)

In the sequence of this Scripture, I found richness I had not known before. I had so often heard the beginning of verse 18, which says, "There is no fear in love, but perfect love casts out fear," but that sentiment fell flat when separated from the rest of the passage. I wondered, "How do I gain hold of that perfect love to cast out my fear?"

When I meditated on the context of this more-famous part of the passage, I found an anchor for those words. The passage begins with "And we have seen and testify." I thought, okay, this is something tangible, something real. Then it continues: "that the Father has sent his Son to be the Savior of the world." Aha! The perfect love is about the One I love! The truth that Jesus came as the Savior of the world. His blood shed to bring clarity. Life. A gorgeous, sure day.

I realized that either I believed this or I wasn't truly a follower of Christ. So in a sense, perfect love was tied to the foundation of everything I believed.

As I appropriated this truth through my major manic episodes in Budapest and Orlando, I found the love I needed. You see, these mental breakdowns seemingly stripped everything away from me. My work. My home. Motherhood. Being a wife. My mind. Yet this passage promised me that if I believed in Jesus as Savior, I was putting myself in God, in perfect love. This perfect love would cast out every fear, every brooding black cloud darkening my vision. That truth, like the entirety of God's truth, could never be destroyed. So I knew there had to be a way to be healed from my fears.

As I opened my arms wide and took this in, I found rest. First, for a moment, then two, then hundreds. I was in the arms of perfect love because of the One on whom I had long ago staked every fiber of my being. I could grasp this from my deepest, innermost places and find a refuge from every storm.

Love as the New Normal

As I endured both hospital stays and fought for life, I knew it would take more than a momentary victory to lead me to the security of God's love. I needed a near-constant reality of God's affection to walk intimately alongside me. It seemed as though love would have to become my breath. But in those days, I could not grasp how to accomplish that.

Gradually, I remembered my story and recalled when I had first gained a deep understanding of God's love. It had been a spring day in 2000, after I had experienced what I now see as my first manic episode, which came more than a decade before the episode that hospitalized me in Hungary. This one involved a week without sleep, no diagnosis or treatment, and the gradual return of a clear, reality-based mind. Although I was not hospitalized, I had endured wild visions and many nights without sleep.

This particular day was warm and bright—the kind of spring day I wanted to receive into my bones. A first-year seminary student, I had walked the campus of Gordon-Conwell Theological Seminary in South Hamilton, Massachusetts, just after turning twenty-six. I stopped to journal and write poetry near the quad as the green trees rustled with a steady breeze. I returned to my apartment and lay down for a touch of sleep, letting it "roll over my eyelids," as my grandmother would say. What followed was a few blessed minutes where I felt wrapped in a love so potent that it was my last thought before I slept and my first thought when I woke.

When I awoke that day, I heard, "It's time to go home." That might not seem like an earth-shattering message. But it was for me at that time. I had been running away from home for a long time. It took the hell of my first major manic episode to bring me to a place of surrender complete enough to say yes to my standing invitation to come home. The calling wrapped itself in precious warmth, which can be described only as the living reality of God's love.

As I moved home to my parents' house in Perkasie, Pennsylvania, and began to heal from my episode and crushing romantic heartbreak, I rediscovered the precious love of my parents. But I also discovered new space where I could rest in the love of God and stop trying to earn it at all. Not only had I been running from my physical home, but I had been striving and performing to somehow gain love. Not anymore. I was now certain that I was loved—by my parents and by God—completely, fully. This love came with an arrow-like goal to help me heal in the deepest places.

In subsequent years, this spiritual space offered little bursts of love, gave me an overwhelming sense of God's intentional care, and guided me through much pain and trial—a wilderness of conflicting circumstances, both inside and outside of me. The fifteen years from my first manic episode until my second, in Hungary, were hedged by God's overwhelming love. Resting in that love became my new normal as I lived with what I didn't know at the time was bipolar disorder.

When my symptoms reemerged in 2015 and again in 2016, this precious peace of divine love took a major hit. But I continued to cling to it, even if all I had was a memory of that peace. I had to know it was still there for me.

We all need this. A restart. An emotional space. A place where we so distinctly feel the nature of God's love. It's essential for any life. We don't need to perform or, really, do anything to get it. It comes to us through the exquisite reality of the God who donned flesh and lived among us. Love came to our world once and for all so we would never have to live without it.

As we let go of our need to strive for the love of God, we prove the perfect love of 1 John 4:18. We find this love is greater than all that would try to come between God and us—especially that which is most primal: fear. We find love that takes form in the arms of the Father around us, the eyes of Christ before us, and the comfort of the Holy Spirit beside us. Because the love of the Trinity is above all, through all, and in all, we hold on to it as our very breath. We hold on to it as he always holds us.

From that spring catnap in the final days of my hard-fought-for life as a seminary student in Massachusetts, I discovered a tangible substance of the love of God that I never wanted to let go. My resolve was severely tested over the years, but I've emerged all the stronger in God's love because of that testing.

Dear one, I believe he longs to show you this dwelling place of love. He longs to hold you beyond the striving, the bottling of a thousand fears, the sense of unworthiness. He has an embrace of perfect affection. Do you have the courage, the faith, to receive it in your heart of hearts?

Keeping the Vision before You

Though we are meant to have love now, it is also a destination we are traveling toward, a place of security, warmth, and infallible love. And we don't have to wonder what environment we will find there or what kind of skies we will see. This place of love is true and unchanging, and all around is beauty. We will receive exactly what we need there.

We will receive our ultimate prize when our journey is done and we're forever safe in God's arms. But he calls us now to travel wholeheartedly toward the vision of love's glory, for which we're eternally made. This is how we must learn to walk, especially those of us who are going through mental illness. Such illnesses are some of the most heinous tactics of the enemy, sucker punches intended to make us doubt that anyone, let alone God, truly loves us.

But no. We fight against the enemy with the vision of God's love before us. We look to Jesus and steady ourselves with his promises, like this one:

> Therefore, since we are surrounded by such a great
> cloud of witnesses, let us throw off everything that
> hinders and the sin that so easily entangles. And let
> us run with perseverance the race marked out for us,
> fixing our eyes on Jesus, the pioneer and perfecter of
> faith. For the joy set before him he endured the cross,
> scorning its shame, and sat down at the right hand of
> the throne of God. (Heb. 12:1–2)

Though not explicitly mentioned in this passage, love is implied throughout, beginning with the *cloud of witnesses,* words that make me remember my mama. She was there in 2000 when I came home in pieces after my manic episode. At one point, she put her arms around me and said, "It's always darkest before the dawn, Abby." The words were anything but cliché coming from her lips. She had endured miscarriages, financial ruin, multiple chronic illnesses, and would soon face terminal cancer. But she never, ever stopped fighting for life, her own being rooted ultimately in God's love. Then, there is my father. I have written in these pages about how my father anchored me in the strong, sovereign, yet Abba love of God, particularly after my hospitalizations. He passed away as I was completing this book, and his constant affection and fervent prayers will be sorely missed. But his eternal imprint upon my life will continue to carry me through whatever comes in my journey on this earth. I know that my parents and my grandparents are in that cloud of witnesses, as are so many loved ones from your life. They are cheering each of us on, whispering, "Don't lose heart, beloved. Keep looking to him."

What does it mean to fix our eyes on Jesus? Henri Nouwen writes,

> This face-to-face experience [of seeing Christ] leads us to the heart of the great mystery of the incarnation. We can see God and live! As we try to fix our eyes on the eyes of Jesus, we know that we are seeing the eyes of God. What greater desire is there in the human heart than to see God?[2]

We fix our eyes on Jesus by fixing our eyes on love, for God is love. He shows himself in every gift given to us, in every act of love toward us, and ultimately in the life of the incarnate God offered for us. He's always singing, even shouting, and at times persistently yet gently whispering, "Look up. I am here. I am love."

In times of intense battle, we must recognize our deepest desire—to be home in God's love. When we seek him and cry out for him, he'll never elude us.

Yet we often don't take those steps because fear is so uncomfortable. It's hard to have the courage to recognize the presence of fear within us. We avoid this knowledge at all costs. We distract ourselves from it. We chase after things that make us feel confident in ourselves and keep us from seeing and naming our fears.

But if we don't truly face our fear, we can't receive our heart's desire in overcoming it. We can't receive the perfect love of God.

As we walk this oft-wearying path from fear to love, Jesus is not only our vision and great champion, but he is also our friend, our shepherd, even our lover. The whole of his life forms our sky, our most true sky, which will illumine our pathway home.

When we really meditate on Jesus's life, on what he went through to win the battle for us, we gain a perspective that outweighs the hellish pain of anything we have endured—or will endure in the future.

I do not use the word *hell* lightly. But when I describe those dark nights of void, the black holes that threatened to swallow me, I say *hell* a lot. I've felt the acute fear of being in the presence of the evil one without being able to detect the presence of God at all. I have faced so many levels of hell and lived to tell my story.

My experiences have all happened for a reason, a beautiful reason: so I can testify to the life of Christ and his life's greatest message. As I have struggled through my dark days, God has shown me that to the degree I have felt fear, to that same degree and far greater I will feel his love. And I don't have to wait for heaven to feel that love; rather, it begins in the now. And he shows me the way.

When we see how great was the love of the Son to the Father, we see that Jesus was never apart from his Father's love throughout all the fear-inducing circumstances of his life—when the chief priests and elders plotted to kill him, when he faced demonic spirits, when the storms raged while he was aboard a fisherman's boat, when he was called to raise a dead man to life. Even in the final hours of his life, when he was agonizing in the garden and begging for the cup to pass him, when he was scourged and a crown of thorns was pressed into his head—in all these events, God's love was perfectly his. He was immense in love, casting aside the fear, as Jesus asked forgiveness for those responsible for his death.

And in the greatest darkness, piercing the eternal skies of the heavens, Jesus cried out, "My God, my God, why have you forsaken me?" (Matt. 27:46). Yet, he overcame and said, "It is finished" (John 19:30). In this declaration, he pronounced victory of the love of the Trinity over the gruesome, consuming center of fear.

This love is calling to you, friend. Do you hear it? He's speaking to you through his Holy Spirit in me. I say this humbly. He let me experience near-death and horrific manic episodes and yet brought me through it all. He has filled me with a greater confidence in his love than I've ever known. He has given me a deeper understanding of and a readier willingness to sacrifice for this love. It's a gift I confidently embrace for myself. And I believe this gift is meant for you, too.

God has the richest and fullest life imaginable prepared for you. He is this good. And no power of evil, no blackness in this world, or even a journey with mental illness can take this away from you. Let him be your true north, pointing you straight to the beauty of his love, his everlasting sky.

8

DANCING AT SUNRISE
From Sorrow to Joy

I lay beside Jared in the dark of night—my mind ravaged by lies. It had been fifteen months since my hospitalization in Budapest, and four days since I had returned from the University Behavioral Center in Orlando. So much had changed in those fifteen months. My children were now enrolled in US schools. We had begun to form new friendships. But my bipolar symptoms were escalating. The dark voices conspired to convince me that I had no hope.

The voices warped my mind so that I fully believed I had destroyed the world for all eternity. They argued that God was not stronger than evil and that Jesus's work was not enough. Most devastating of all, they told me that my husband, the best man I had ever known, had married an evil woman. I felt utterly detached from my children, unable to draw them close. I was certain I had wrecked their lives forever.

A Million Pieces

Those intense days after my hospitalization were an exceedingly dark and sorrowful period. It was as if the radiant sky was hidden from me under a thick blackness. My beloved name, Abigail, which means "my father is joy," seemed like a cruel joke.

I tried. I really tried to pick up the pieces and make some sense of my life. But my life at that moment resembled a crumbling mosaic, and I ached at everything that was broken. It seemed nothing in my life could be mended. Even my memories were fragmented.

I wanted to move from my gaping sorrow to the abundant joy I believed ought to mark my life, but I did not know how. Eventually, I arrived at what felt like a shocking contradiction. I sensed God leading me to embrace my darkest days, encouraging me to enter them, with him, rather than seeking an escape through a book or a movie.

When my life didn't seem to be leading me anywhere, I put my hand in Jesus's own scarred hand and allowed him to lead me deeper into the darkness. I could do this because I knew he was the light, which could not be overcome.

He took me to the waves of my sorrow. I entered the places of deep sadness and looked at how I felt I had abandoned my children. It had not happened only in the past fifteen months; it had started earlier. My lack of diagnosis, my depression, and my anxiety symptoms had led me to withdraw from my kids. Missed opportunities to play, to run together in parks, to read stories at bedtime—all haunted me.

I flinched in the face of it, but he kept hold of my hand and spoke his love song over me. He showed the ways and times I *had* been present for my children: shooting hoops with my son, holding tea parties with my daughter, building blocks on the floor with my youngest, attending school performances. Though the darkness was great, there were still beautiful images shining through my life as a mother. What would be redeemed was far greater as I embraced the grace apportioned to me as a wife and mother.

It was important to travel to the place of my sorrow. While it hurt to relive my gaping absences, it was helpful to realize that they were not the whole story.

Ann Voskamp, in her beautiful book *One Thousand Gifts*, describes thoughts of gratitude as nails we drive through wood, making them true.[1] This is what it felt like. One pound of the hammer at a time, one feeling of gratitude at a time, I would bring my thoughts into a strong, clear path toward God and his evident love. Thankfulness is the great healer.

Music had always been a source of strength and joy in my life. But after my hospitalization in Hungary, songs of thankfulness became consistent medicine for my soul. The lyrics gave me the courage to endure the grueling process of working out my salvation.

Over time, I became more content as I realized that the destruction of what I had been was so thorough that I would never be able to pick up those million pieces again. But beyond that destruction there was a goodness, a new life to be forged from the pieces, built fully upon God and his redemption.

Over the months after my second hospitalization, as I gradually entered the pain and torture of my mental illness journey, specifically the spiraling out of reality and into believing lie was truth, I realized something extraordinary. If I would let him, God could redeem even those lies and shine his light, which would refract a million radiant colors. Not only *could* he, but he longed to do this. His desire was to remake those million pieces of my story so they were shot through with his light.

Furthermore, because I had struggled so much, I could more fully appreciate his returning me to joy, beginning with each renewed thought. With my change, I could also embody a compassion that could change the lives of many. The change would come as I trusted his truth, beyond the lies, and let him create a new thing through my life.

It wasn't going to be an easy trip, but I now saw a path before me. One thought at a time, I would supplant the darkness and see the overcoming light born anew into radiant joy. I began this journey even as my hands shook from new medicines. Soon, my breakthrough anxiety would make my feet—and sometimes my whole body—shake so badly that I couldn't drive on the highway. No, the path would not be easy, but I had to believe it was possible.

In the Crushing

The song "New Wine" from Hillsong Worship begins:

> In the crushing
> In the pressing
> You are making
> New wine . . .[2]

Jesus talked about how there was a need for "new wineskins" with new wine (Matt. 9:17). The old wineskins would no longer suffice because the new wine would bust them wide open. In the same way, I had to let go of what I thought my life was supposed to be, the old wineskins, and embrace the reality of entirely new wineskins, along with the new wine they would hold.

But crushing and pressing are involved in making new wine. On the heels of a very real crushing of my mind—two of them, in fact—I was facing a continued need for surrendered sorrow, a different kind of crushing and pressing, in order to fully produce this new wine. It all felt so disappointing. Then, I remembered my story, back to the early days.

My early elementary report cards were lined with "Outstanding" rankings, marred by one "Needs Improvement" blot on my second-grade report card. It was for "Handles Disappointment." Many were the tears of my young days, whether shed behind a textbook during school, on the sideline of a field hockey or lacrosse game, or in a fit of wailing upon my bed. I did not handle disappointment well.

Disappointment crushes. All too often, it can breed cynicism and end dreams. This has happened to me, and never more intensely than when we had to leave our life in Hungary. But in the crushing, I kept hearing God whisper fervently, "Endure, beloved, endure." Amid all the evil whispers I was hearing during my manic episode in Orlando, I also heard this: "Endure." I didn't know what the message meant except that I should keep fighting for true life in my belief that God was real despite all the lies. I was pressed hard, and this very real pressing held excruciating sorrow. So often, I just felt the pain. All I could do was seek to hang on to the overarching narrative of Christ's redemption. This great story would win in my life and in all things.

Sometimes, dear reader, this is all we can do. With something like mental illness, when our minds are sponges for lies, we have to trust the greater truth of God. He is present beyond every weight of crushing, making new wine. And not just any wine, but full-bodied, rich, exquisite wine that will one day be served at the great feast of God in the new heaven and new earth.

As we walk this long road home, there may be many times God calls us to simply endure. We may be in a season of great sorrow, with life crushing in on us, but God may be *allowing* us to be crushed. Every single one of our beliefs may be tested, but in this pressing down hard, our deepest truths can come to life. We are made for God, and he will have us forever, basking in the beauty of his love, his fullness in the heavens. Moreover, this new wine he is making of us will bear the stunning story of his beauty replacing the ashes of our sorrow.

Clinging to Truth

We must cling to the truth that we are made for the joy of God as we journey in this life. We can't let it go because we are designed for it. And if we lay hold of the truth of God, we will indeed be victorious.

I had to learn that there was always a greater truth, even greater than what mental illness was speaking of me. I was a very long time in the crushing and pressing, and it hurt so badly. It felt as though no one could understand. In my worst times, God felt so distant that I doubted even he could understand.

But that changed one hot, hot, Florida June day, weeks after my hospital stay in Orlando. I was painting an entryway bench in our new house, trying to brush life into this place. I was listening to a sermon when, almost inadvertently, I had an "aha" moment. I recognized the hideous source behind all the millions of lies I had heard: the clear, determined face of the ancient enemy.

When we can really see this primordial serpent, Satan, behind the things happening to us—whether in mind, body, soul, or circumstances—his hand is tipped. We can remember with clarity how to fight—and how to win.

Eve must have heard many lies after the Fall. The enemy, proud in triumph, would have been relentless with her, telling her how she had destroyed the world forever. God remained close, watchful, but not in the guarded perfection she had previously known. And the enemy surely took advantage in this yawning cavern.

Humans have lived in this vein of susceptibility to the enemy's scheming, lying ways since the Fall. When perfection with God lay in ruins, there Satan was, wielding great power from his kingdom of darkness.

But looking with the eyes of faith, we can see him. Jesus. Reaching back through time with one hand and forward to the end of all things with the other, saying, as he did on the cross, "It is finished" (John 19:30). Although he has not yet returned to bring all his beloved brothers and sisters to their promised home in the new heaven and the new earth, he will. It is not in question. He will have final say over the perspective of all time and eternity. When we behold him and the skies of heaven, we will find gorgeous, fully saturated rainbows of fulfilled promises, sunrises of newness, sunsets of completion, and starry nights of a million illuminations in all directions. We'll gaze forever upon it all. There will be no need for sun or lamp for he will be all the glory (Rev. 22:5).

In the following days, as I continued working on the entryway bench and pressed into this realization of Jesus's victory over all time and eternity, I realized I had a choice in everything. I could choose whether or not to believe this final and forever

A MILLION SKIES

homecoming is true, truer than the lies or darkness. God's Spirit seemed to be leading me to answer ultimate questions:

- What did I finally believe to be true?
- Was there a greater picture to my life?
- Could I find joy in the new day?

As we each seek to cling to truth, can we look in the mirror and voice the reality of who we are in God? For us, this can mean first recognizing the extraordinary nature of the power of God's love. His love is like the deep magic of Narnia, which raises Aslan after the White Witch kills him in her grotesque ritual.[3] Next, we must recognize the ordinary nature of God's love. We receive God's goodness thousands of times in the day. When we rest in this extraordinary, ordinary, abiding goodness, we will find our hearts firmly melded to the truth.

Trading Mourning for Dancing

We mourn in our sorrow and sadness. But Isaiah 61:3 declares Jesus has come to give "the oil of joy instead of mourning." He provides what we need to journey from sorrow to joy "for all the promises of God find their Yes in [Jesus]" (2 Cor. 1:20 ESV).

Yet, the process of opening ourselves up to such joy is not easy. I have spent some time defining this process of changing my thoughts and reorienting my emotions so they are fixed on truth. I like to name three "steps" that work to renew our hearts and restore right thinking.

Reignite. Here, we deal with our "why" for reorienting our thoughts and emotions. We believe anew that our despair, doubt, and sorrow can be transformed to hope and faith with an out-working of joy. This reignition of positive emotions happens as

124

we recognize that our motivation to live joyfully, lightheartedly includes the love of others in our lives—both their love for us and our love for them. Because we want to see their healing related to our journey of mental illness, we ignite our inner desire for change. More importantly, we recognize it is God's will for us to return to—or experience for the first time—true joy. His relentless love is our greatest motivator to move from sorrow to joy.

Rewire. By examining what we are thinking, we can deal with the pattern of our thoughts and change how they begin and end. For example, we may be allowing our thought patterns to be defined by a lie, such as, "I have a debilitating, shameful mental illness, therefore I am unworthy of love." This thought pattern leads to negative emotions such as shame, self-hatred, and more. We must find the inner clarity to recognize and identify what we are thinking, and then we can choose to rewire our thought patterns to begin and end with truth. We replace the lie with something like, "I am made in God's image and the object of God's redemption; therefore, I am worthy of his love and all true love that can be given." We choose to undertake this process, and as we do, our emotions come into line with the truth so that we can experience emotions like real joy.

Refill. We move to fill our thoughts with overflowing positive emotions found in the love of God. As I described in Chapter Seven, we can fill our brains with God's Word like we fill our lungs with the air we breathe. We fill our thoughts with God's promises and believe he keeps those promises. Dwell on portions of Scripture like Jeremiah 31:3: "I have loved you with an everlasting love; I have drawn you with unfailing kindness." Or Colossians 1:13–14: "[God] has rescued us from the dominion of darkness and brought us into the kingdom of the Son he loves, in whom we have redemption, the forgiveness of sins." When these promises become our truth, we will see our emotions opened to a new life, a freshness, that cannot be contained.

I share these three steps with a bit of trepidation because I fear you may experience a sense of failure if you are not able to use these techniques to transform your thoughts and emotions. For me, not finding success when using these steps is a sign that I need professional and peer help. Maybe one of my medications isn't working properly, or some past trauma is surfacing that I cannot handle. Or, maybe even a herculean effort to lift myself up is just not producing results. When that happens, I know I need to get on the phone or in a counselor's office and get help with this part of my struggle.

There should always be a tension between reaching for outside help and looking within and to God for help. While medication and therapy can help us regain balance, no one can work through the experience of our sorrow for us. The battle for our joy is ultimately won in faith in the life, death, and resurrection of the one who became our sorrow. In his journey to the depths of pain, he made a way for us to experience his presence. By understanding that he is with us, we can know true, abiding joy.

There are days when I feel weary of my battle for joy. I wish it weren't such a difficult fight. But knowing the depth of our sorrow can help us experience the opposite degree of the joy of God. When I think of all that God saved me from in the ravages of mental illness, I experience a joy so profound it nearly knocks me over. It is not a childlike joy, though I definitely have those moments. It is also not a fluffy "don't worry; be happy" kind of joy. My joy has matured into something that can anchor me even in the overwhelming waves of sadness this life can bring.

As I mentioned in Chapter Seven, I lost my dear father in August of 2021, while I was completing this book. There have been few sorrows like losing my daddy, who prayed me through every storm "in the strong name of King Jesus," as he liked to end his prayers. When he was fading and too weak to pray in his usual way, I felt the pull toward an abyss of sorrow. But God stepped in. He has given me joy amid very real sorrow because I am confident my father now knows everlasting joy. Our God of joy is ever greater than the sorrows that are part and parcel of this life. And the heaven of God breaks through in our losses to give us stunning glimpses of our God's indestructible, gorgeous, forever sky.

Friend, this can be your experience too. Out of my anchoring joy, I am praying right now that you will begin to know your own deep, consistent, and profound joy. And in the depths of this joy, may you find the steady feet to dance.

9

THE BEAUTY OF STILLNESS
From War to Peace

February 2015

I could not sleep. Day after day. Week after week. In this state, I deteriorated as I processed delusions and visions. Before me, a war was raging day and night at every level in the heavens. Soaring angels and terrifying beasts. God and Satan. Saints on gleaming white horses. One evening I felt myself in the pit of hell surrounded by gruesome demons. I could feel my flesh on fire, and the heat and sulfur stench choked my every breath. I writhed in pain and cried out for relief. When the vision passed, the sheer terror left me trembling.

The trauma shattered the beauty, creativity, and peace my mind had once known. I became a shell of myself, and I longed for sanity. After two weeks of battling this onslaught at home, I was admitted into the mental ward of the hospital in Budapest, but the visions remained. They were all horrifyingly real to me—even more real than my home, my family, and my God.

The Battle

I fought against what I was seeing in my compromised mental state, battling to regain what I had once known as reality. But time and again, the spiritual realm it seemed I had entered presented itself to be what was entirely true.

One night before entering the hospital, I had a vision of the Antichrist. Gray and slimy with bloodshot eyes and veins on the outside of his body, he stood between me and his innocent victims. Each was tied to a chair, while he hissed lies about their worth, his tongue reaching into their ears. Within me, a fierce, righteous anger rose up, and I was drawn into the story, shouting, "You will not have them, they are of the light and beloved of God and you will release them!"

Later I saw three witches speaking incantations over me and other women who were also tied to chairs. Their haunting chants were muttered over a misty caldron.

I tried to explain these battle scenes to those I knew in our ministry, but no one would listen. Tormented mentally, I cried and pled with those around me to understand the dire situation of these women and me. In my compromised, sleep-deprived state, I lacked the credibility to prove my visions were true.

In a frenzied state, I phoned our mentor, Dan, in the middle of the night and told him I had seen the Antichrist and the end was coming. He struggled to determine whether I was truly having a spiritual experience or experiencing a chemical imbalance and mental instability. I couldn't see objectively what was happening to me, and I wept inside because I couldn't make anyone see the fierce war portrayed in my visions.

Because I could not convince others that what I was seeing was real, I withdrew, slipping further and further into these vivid, apocalyptic scenes.

Scenes from the second half of the book of Revelation marched before my eyes. I saw a woman dressed in red, Babylon the Great, the prostitute depicted in chapters 14, 16, and 17. Along with her, I saw the minions of darkness rearrange the story so that Babylon, the Beast, and the False Prophet triumphed, and the whole of heaven and earth were subject to their eternal torment. I believed I had to fight to keep intact the biblical version of the Revelation story. At one point, I read in a loud voice portions of the story, and I was willing the rider on a white horse to victory. I fully believed I had to carry out a mission to preserve the cosmos for God.

However, I grew weaker and weaker, my defenses obliterated from lack of sleep. I used every reserve to fight the battle I believed God had chosen me to fight in the heavens, but I could stand less and less against the evil I saw. I felt powerless and weak as my strength waned.

Things had so run away from me that I believed I would be delivered into a prostitution ring through the hospital in Budapest. As I was admitted, it seemed I was being fully given over to evil, and I heard the foulest things and saw the end of the world in the most gruesome nightmare with Lucifer winning, not God. This torturous mental roller coaster made me frantic to leave the hospital.

There was no rhyme or reason for such a derailing of my mind. It hurt everyone who knew me and saw me like this. It nearly took me from life mentally. During my first week in the hospital, I felt I was battling to keep my mind. I feared I would live out my days on earth out of touch with reality, fully isolated in my mental prison, unable to be freed into my life as a wife and mother.

The stakes were so high. I knew this was a life-and-death battle, one way or the other. I felt the weight of it with every breath I took, every vision I saw, every terrorizing thought I endured.

Losing It All

It is difficult to form words to describe the sheer heaviness of those days. Everything seemed to be of monumental importance. What I was "seeing" or "hearing" had urgent meaning. I needed to understand and make others understand.

Even after things moved toward "normal," I continued to feel the effects of so much mental trauma. It was as though the chemical imbalance had ravaged my mind, leaving behind the blown-up bridges and demolished streets of a devastated war zone. How would I, how could I, move toward true stability?

Battle scars wove themselves through my mind. Gardens of happy things had been uprooted by the cruel hand of mental illness. I could not trust my own thoughts. Healing often felt out of my control.

I felt out of control and fragile for months after my hospitalization in Hungary and again during and after my manic episode in Orlando. I experienced many similar apocalyptic delusions and visions as I was admitted to UBC, like I was fighting the second part of the mental war that had begun in Hungary.

The sheer trauma of each hospital stay overwhelmed me. I felt like a baby after each episode, trying to learn how to breathe, eat, and walk again. And I couldn't escape the thought that my mind was untrustworthy. After I returned from Hungary, my friend Jess, who works in the mental health field, said simply, "It's so hard when you can't trust your mind." It was anguish of the deepest kind to know I had to rebuild my entire life, one thought at a time.

Although I eventually did achieve a great victory, I also had to accept that my mind was susceptible to illness. Becoming out of touch with my mind was not a "once and done" thing. It could, and did, happen again. I realized I needed a path to mental wholeness. The lies could and would seek to suck me into sick patterns of thinking, so I had to build my defenses.

One Brick at a Time

I knew I needed truth upon truth to remake my war-wracked mind. So, I began to construct my defenses brick by brick against the would-be onslaught of lies and lingering paranoia.

I desperately needed to lay a solid foundation. The apostle Paul told the church in Philippi to think about "whatever is true, whatever is noble, whatever is right, whatever is pure, whatever is lovely, whatever is admirable . . . excellent or praiseworthy" (Phil. 4:8). I needed to put these kinds of thoughts at the base of my mind, and it wasn't an easy task.

There were no quick fixes here. I had to stand guard and keep watch over what I was thinking about. More importantly, I needed to remember that God was guarding me. So I called my beloved, prayer warrior father often. Sleep was still elusive in the days following my stay at UBC, and fear hung about the corners of my mind, so, as I shared before, my father prayed with fervor for the Lord's complete, sufficient care for me: "God, you own her, and you own her forever." I grew stronger in my inner being.

This truth, affirmed through my father's prayer, became like a cornerstone in the reconstruction of my mind. In my times without sleep, when my mind was full of visions, delusions, and awful untruths, I had been told that Satan, not God, owned me. My beloved father's prayer was a stake in the ground, reclaiming the territory of my mind for God and his kingdom.

Calming the Waters

During my mental war, another battle was being fought. My loved ones, who believe in the goodness of God, were praying me back to health. From the very beginning of my struggles in the ICU in Hungary, people started to pray. During my darkest days there, these warriors battled for me, pleading for me.

As God's people rallied on my behalf, the heart of God moved and visited me with his peace. It came as the tiniest illumination in my alternate reality, but I began to believe that peace was truer than anything else I had seen or experienced throughout my episode. My inner peace began as God's hand touched my mind through the sunlight streaming in the thick-paned window when I awoke in the ICU. It continued as we relocated to the United States and as people continued to pray.

When the battle was raging in my mind, God used the intercession of others to bring me calm. Their prayers served as a reservoir that quenched my thirst when the battle was at its worst. When I had nothing left, these prayers lifted me and gave me strength. It is always necessary to have people who will pray for us, be for us. We cannot survive a journey of mental illness without this reinforcement.

But there are also battles that no one else can fight. We must find the strength to claim victory and move toward the calm of a stormless sky. Although prayers and encouragement from others can give us a vital boost, nothing can replace our communion with God. Throughout my journey with mental illness, I have found this living relationship with God, learning to move to his rhythm, the most essential part of my battle plan.

Our peace, friends, is not a Band-Aid—a flimsy thing that can peel away. No, God is our peace.

We can picture ourselves with the disciples on that raging sea (Mark 4:37–38). We share their fear, their doubts, the belief they would be overcome by this storm. We can imagine our Master asleep on the boat and asking, "Doesn't he care?" We each can live faithless in this place, not truly knowing the manifest heart of our God.

However, on our road toward mental health, we must grow a much deeper faith. We need to place our whole selves within the refuge of God. As we do this, we will see the Savior wake and speak to our storms with the pure confidence of God: "Peace! Be still" (Mark 4:39 ESV). The raging stops, and the sea becomes smooth as glass.

Practically, sometimes, we become tired and wonder, "Why are these lies here again?" But we cannot lose heart, for we know he has overcome the world (John 16:33). This means he has defeated all that would seek to pull us back into the lies. We must dwell in the truth that resonates from the prophet Isaiah's words, "You keep him in perfect peace whose mind is stayed on you because he trusts in you" (Isa. 26:3 ESV).

Twenty years ago, a friend said she always felt peace when she was around me. This was a beautiful declaration to be internalized. Yet after my hospitalizations in Hungary and Orlando, I wondered if I would ever know that peace again.

When my father prayed for me after I was released from the hospital in 2016, he referenced my being under "the wing of God." It reminded me of the first verses of Psalm 91.

> Whoever dwells in the shelter of the Most High
>> will rest in the shadow of the Almighty.
> I will say of the LORD, "He is my refuge and my fortress,
>> my God, in whom I trust."
> Surely he will save you
>> from the fowler's snare
>> and from the deadly pestilence.
> He will cover you with his feathers,
>> and under his wings you will find refuge;
>> his faithfulness will be your shield and rampart. (vv. 1–4)

I began to meditate on this psalm over and over again, returning repeatedly to the images of God's shelter, his what-could-only-be enormous shield of warmth, his refuge and fortress, and his covering me with the feathers of his wings. I felt secure here as I clung to him like my very life depended on it—because it did.

We can see that faithfulness is mentioned in Psalm 91 because God is so very faithful.

In October of 2020, as I was preparing for a writing retreat where I would work on this book, some lies I thought were forever defeated were trying to mess with my mind. My dear friend Kelley, who prays for me regularly, prayed for me in this battle. She saw a huge wing covering me as the sun shone down. I felt the warmth of that picture both figuratively and in my body. I remembered God's faithfulness in my journey, my father's anchoring prayer, and this friendship with a prayer warrior like Kelley—and recognized them as gifts to see me safe into God's arms one day and forever.

The image of a refuge or shelter can be incredibly stabilizing. Heather Holleman writes, "Through the pages of Scripture, we meet a God who rescues us and keeps us in his guarding care."[1] The One who is in all, above all, and through all things is a living shelter. A refuge against the storm because he made the storm. Nothing can touch God and his supreme grandeur. As the prophet Isaiah declares, "The LORD is exalted, for he dwells on high; he will fill Zion with justice and righteousness, and he will be the stability of your times, abundance of salvation, wisdom, and knowledge; the fear of the LORD is Zion's treasure" (33:5–6 ESV). In this promise of him as "the stability of [my] times," I could see confirmation of a deepening anchor of trust.

This stability is especially important for us to hold on to as we weather the deep water of trials. The lessons I learned through this teaching have helped me stay grounded in the face of the vivid memories of fierce manic episodes. In my delusions and visions, the greatness of God, his sovereignty, omniscience, and power were strategically attacked. Evil had a field day in my mind. In my heart, I didn't believe God was less. Rather, I believed my sin and what I thought was complicit agreement with the enemy were too much for a holy God to overlook. Most terrorizing was believing, in my compromised state, that God had forsaken his world, his plan of redemption.

You see how we must begin at the very deepest level of our minds and its integrated places of heart and soul. When truth comes, faith marries it again. I embraced things I had known before, and now, in my mental nakedness after the mania had stripped me bare, these promises clothed me with warmth and protection, so completely, so fully.

I had known God's truths before my manic episodes, but I came to comprehend the truth more deeply because of my mental war. Through mental illness, God had revealed a beautiful paradox and worked his healing. He set me free to a life of peace.

I believe he can use your deepest pains in the same way. As we journey on, we discover not only calming waters, but also the presence of God himself.

Precious Is the Peace

This calming reality restored my greatest physical loss: sleep. While it was horrific to go without sleep for weeks at a time, I can be so thankful now for the gift of sleep.

When I am in a pattern of not sleeping, I experience a lot of anxiety as I try to go to sleep. In my bad periods, my mind just couldn't calm down. It would cycle around and around with the same thoughts. When I would start to drift off, my mind would resume whirling. It was torturous in the worst moments, terrorizing too.

But God. God pursued me with sweet sleep. At first, it was just minutes, tiny naps that were little gifts to help me believe in the promise of more. When I first came out of the hospital in Hungary, I would take Benadryl. I lay in bed and tried to sleep, whether it was bedtime or not. When I slept, I would rejoice. Then, I could receive God's peace each time, more and more.

However, peace is not an easy journey for me, or any of us. In those fifteen months between my hospital stays, I was only able to get four to five solid hours through a sleeping pill. Because I didn't want to become addicted to the medicine, I tried to wean myself off it. It did not go well. My sleep was in a very tenuous place, making me susceptible to another bout of mania.

As I fought through my manic episodes, I was sucked into the visions because I felt I needed to complete a special mission. I felt burdened by the need to fulfill God's will, which is the antithesis of peace. But I couldn't break out of it. Hence, no sleep, no peace.

As I write this book five years later, I am in such a profoundly different place that I can only fall on my knees in thankfulness. As I came through my episode in Orlando, God spoke to my heart, again and again, that I had endured a severe attack on my person and that I was an overcomer who would live to tell my story. And I would be known, once again, as a person who lived peace.

How did I get to this place of such peace that I sleep so easily now? The short answer is God. The long answer is God. The everything-in-between answer is God.

Peace has been the lilt of his love song over me. I gaze on him, the one who quiets me by his love (Zeph. 3:17 ESV), known ultimately in Christ, and his promise to be all that I need. My testimony has been that as I look to him, I find him and his peace, and long for more of it, so I look to him more, until this peace weaves all throughout my mental landscape.

It is so good to remember childlike faith. An early set of verses I memorized was Philippians 4:6-7, as I wrote them on an index card. "Do not be anxious about anything, but in every situation, by prayer and petition, with thanksgiving, present your requests to God. And the peace of God, which transcends all understanding, will guard your hearts and your minds in Christ Jesus."

I can testify that out of chaos and the war upon my mind, I have found this "peace which transcends all understanding." There was no guarantee I would come through two hospitalizations with the ability to function well as a wife, mother, or woman. But I have. Even more, I have come to thrive in many ways.

After the trauma, anxiety is so close, but God's promise of peace remains closer. The prophet Elijah, after his great spiritual victory and the subsequent upheaval of fleeing for his life, found God as the one who supernaturally prepared food for him while he slept and gave him the strength to go to a place where he could hear his "gentle whisper" (1 Kings 19:3–12). He found God as Peace.

We can each share similar testimonies as we lean into his faithfulness. In some ways, I believe God let my story be dramatic so that I could speak into yours. Near-death experiences, ravages of mental illness, traumatic hospital treatment, and international moves are all part of my story. What is yours?

What wars have you fought through your own mental illness? Do you see yourself in what I have written? Have you been through an actual war? Have you suffered abuse? Are you so lonely you are hearing the torturous lies? Here, I give you the words of the apostle Paul:

> Who shall separate us from the love of Christ? Shall tribulation, or distress, or persecution, or famine, or nakedness, or danger, or sword? As it is written,
>> "For your sake we are being killed all the day long;
>> we are regarded as sheep to be slaughtered."
> No, in all these things we are more than conquerors through him who loved us. For I am sure that neither death nor life, nor angels nor rulers, nor things present nor things to come, nor powers, nor height nor depth, nor anything else in all creation, will be able to

separate us from the love of God in Christ Jesus our Lord. (Rom. 8:35–39 ESV)

Where God's love abides, so does his peace. Just as nothing—I mean nothing—can separate us from the love of God, neither can anything separate us, truly, from his peace. I do not say this in a platitude kind of way. In those days of manic episodes, horror-film reels of delusions and visions, and sinister lies, I absolutely believed I could be separated from God's love and therefore, his peace. But no. God is always writing the better story. The redeemed story.

Friend, begin to name the things that you feel are separating you from God. Ask him to show you what lies you believe about you, or him. Hear him say, "Peace, be still" to the raging storm around your rocking boat. Know that he is enough for all of it.

Maybe your anxiety, your warring mind, is dwelling on all the uncertainty in our world. I understand. I have struggled with world events like the COVID-19 epidemic, racial injustice, political divisiveness. Each has threatened to send me into relapse, but I know that I know a better way, a true way. It is the path of peace, which beholds a faithful, all-powerful, saving God.

Let thoughts that begin in anxiety end in peace. He is waiting to embrace you with the serenity of his arms. He is speaking his peace *beyond all understanding* into you.

Jesus understands fully what it is to be in the midst of a world of upheaval. He took on flesh and entered political unrest so profound it terrorized the world around him. His first followers faced persecution in the Roman arena under the Emperor Nero.[2] His peace is meant to survive anything thrown at it—war, death, famine, and the like.

He longs to wrap us tight as he brings us home to his new heaven and earth. He created you and this world for his glory, the manifestation of his person, his shalom, and he wants us to reflect that peace both now and always.

Let's form a ring of peace around this world as we each behold he who is peace. Let's believe together that mental illness or any other tragedy or hardship is no match for the power of his peace. Let's begin a new chapter, written upon a sky so glorious that we cannot look away.

10

ALL TURNS GOLDEN
From Suffering to Redemption

I had just graduated from college and was full of the fresh beauty of surrender to God and his plans in my life. I had met the man I thought I would marry and felt so full of hope for a life together with him. When the church I attended during college asked me to share my testimony, I passionately described how I wanted to be a part of his kingdom work. I felt a clear call through mind, body, heart, and soul with all the fervor of a twentysomething. I had no way of knowing what testing, what suffering lay ahead.

In a few short years, my relationship ended with the shattering heartbreak of unrequited love. Even worse, the man I loved soon married another. This painful loss was the first of several setbacks that greatly challenged my belief in God's goodness and sufficiency for my life.

In the spring of 2000, I entered my first undiagnosed manic episode just a week after I learned that the man I had wanted to marry was engaged to someone else. That manic experience forced me to abandon my dream of a seminary degree, and two months later I was on my way home to my parents, leaving everything in shambles behind me.

Less than two years after I returned from Massachusetts and Gordon-Conwell seminary to the Pennsylvania of my childhood, I lost my mother to cancer. My grief was compounded by my disappointment that my fervent prayers for her healing had not been answered. The blatant *no* to my pleas for my mother's health dealt a blow to my already weakened faith in God's desire to redeem my suffering and the suffering of those I loved.

Five years after my mother died, while still grieving for this central person in my life, I became both a new mother and a new missionary. Trying to find joy as a mom without my own mother was a new kind of suffering. In the months after my first child was born, I added to this the wretched pain of self-doubt as I struggled with my identity as a mom, a wife, and a missionary. My weariness was compounded by the prolonged exile I described in Chapter Four.

In the next five years, I bore two more children as we continued mission work in the United States, made short-term mission trips to Hungary, and spent two years preparing to move to Hungary full-time. We had been living in Hungary for almost three years by the time of my mental breakdown in February 2015. Every last wall of security, even my reputation of being capable of mere living as a young wife, a mother, a missionary, came crashing down about me. My dignity was stripped, too, as I was strapped to the cold iron of a foreign hospital bed. That twentysomething girl would never have believed such wreckage was even possible.

After my hospitalization and return to the States, I began my prolonged healing journey. As I sought wholeness, I noticed how all my life seemed marked by suffering. When had I not experienced the pelting blows of great hardship? I thought about the hopeful young woman who had stood in front of her church and testified to her intentions of following God no matter what came. Her words felt so foreign to my current experience.

Refined by Fire

When I left Hungary, I was in the midst of the fiery trial that sometimes seemed to consume all of me. I wondered what I might become, and the prospects made my heart grow cold. Everything that my family had worked so hard to build seem to burn down before my eyes. Our dreams and hopes were all pointing toward many more years living, ministering, and raising our family in Hungary. We were establishing ourselves with new friends in a thriving ministry. Jared was able to traverse the city on subway, bus, or tram and initiate spiritual conversations as much as he wanted. It felt like God had been preparing us for this very life.

Although we endured hardship and I struggled, I fully believed we would come through these experiences stronger and more equipped for this life to which we had been called. Then, "poof!" in rapid succession I lost touch with reality and had to be hospitalized. We had to leave quickly and could not return. We had been living in Hungary or preparing to live in Hungary for the past decade. What happened to those ten years, to all we had built?

In 2015, during those beginning days and months on the path of healing, I wrestled with God and found no easy answers. My first instinct was to blame myself. I was the reason we had lost so much. Our dramatic exit from the mission field was my fault.

Yet, the refining hand of God prevailed on my life. I want to make it clear here that it has never been an easy process. No. Day in and day out, it was a battle. Even today, at times, in the memories, the soul agony lingers.

As I walked through such dramatic refining, I was somewhat encouraged just to be alive because I knew I could have died in Hungary. I didn't need the life I had planned for, I just needed one breathing, "I am alive!" kind of life.

Living in the fire forces us to think about God's purpose for our lives. We can gain some insight by looking more closely at the process for refining metals. A blacksmith heats gold until it melts in a flame. Then he stirs and separates the impurities, the dross, from the metal.

When God does this kind of work with us, we can feel this refining in our soul bones. In many ways, we become like molten metal, feeling nothing is solid as the Master Refiner skims away layer after layer of dross. This dross in our lives is like the false worship I discussed in Chapter Four—the act of running after everything but God. When all the things that comfort us are stripped away, we find true, purified worship.

When I was younger, we sang the worship song *Refiner's Fire*. We would call for God to purify our hearts as gold or precious silver. Then we would sing the chorus: "Refiner's fire, My heart's one desire / Is to be holy set apart for you Lord / Ready to do your will."[1]

My younger self had no idea what this song could mean, but my forty-year-old self has experienced this refinement as a wife, mother, and missionary going through a fierce battle with mental illness. Would I have chosen to sing those words as a college student if I had known what my refinement could mean? Although the answer to that question has not always been plain, today I confidently say *yes*.

Surrendering the Whys

In my heart of hearts, I know I will always choose whatever comes if I know it comes from the hand of God. I could lose all things, but I could not lose him and survive. I learned young the vastness of God, his sovereignty, his goodness, his holiness, and his faithfulness. I could no sooner deny him than I could deny the very ground I walk on, the world I know, the heavens above, and the spirit within me.

Surrender to God is the only choice for us on this road of purification. He is worthy of the laying down, the giving up, of all things. He is worthy of every part of our lives. The obedient, good Christian girl that I was knew this. The good Christian woman that I am knows this.

But there is more. God does not want obedience only—he wants our hearts. We must all come to a place where we surrender what we don't understand. This means giving up our "whys" as we struggle to understand hardships that seem to serve no purpose.

I had lots of whys. Why did we have to leave Hungary in the midst of a beautiful ministry? Why did I have to lose my reputation with others because of my mental illness? Why was my battle so intense that I needed multiple medicines to stabilize? Why did my husband and children have to suffer because of my illness?

Because questions like these cause us to be uncomfortable, we can run straight to stock answers. But trying to give shallow answers to these deep questions does an injustice to the very real suffering housed within them. The only true answer is to surrender. Yes, we can sometimes see how God's allowance of bad things can bring good. But, rather than continuing to demand answers to our whys or trying to twist events to fit preconceived answers, the better choice is to simply release the questions into God's hands.

As we do this, our well of compassion toward others is deepened. We are able to sit with them in their pain instead of jumping to answer their whys. With them, we can surrender to God our own need to make sense of it all.

As we move from questions to surrender, we allow space for true lament, which is defined as "a passionate expression of grief."[2] We are able not only to grieve our own brokenness, but also the brokenness of others and the world. In so doing, we sense our heart growing and stretching toward an understanding of the vast heart of God.

God is present in suffering in a way that allows us to be present within it. Jesus wept at Lazarus's grave, even though he knew he was about to bring him back to life. He entered the pain of Mary of Bethany as she wondered why her brother died. He didn't give her a quick answer but met her lament with his own.

As we enter the process of surrender, it is necessary to remain present with our suffering. We cannot truly surrender all we do not understand if we will not get close to the heart of the pain. We must find the freedom to cry out, to mourn, to be honest in the whole of our messy emotion. When we do this, we create space to experience the deep wounding of our suffering, even as we move toward surrender.

After my episodes in Hungary and Orlando, I would sometimes just lay on my bed and feel such deep sorrow, such agony at what had been lost. As I did, I felt the compassion of God embrace me. That compassion allowed me to make the deeper and deeper soul movements toward surrender.

Friend, I want you to hear me that none of this is easy or even straightforward. Our surrender is a process, and we have to stay the course. We must engage in a moment-to-moment fight to not turn our backs on God or on our belief that he is still good. Sometimes all we can do is breathe in and out because the pain is so real and we are so confused about why we have to go through mental illness or any other life-altering hardship. In those moments, it's good to voice our questions, for in the voicing we find a God who cares, with the glisten of tears in his eyes, as he holds us—even if he doesn't answer our whys. Knowing he cares shows us we can surrender our questions because he is worthy of our surrender.

Part of a Greater Story

As we journey this long road, our stories weave into the fabric of God's redemptive plan, but we can see the underside only; the knots lack cohesiveness, so we can't make out the pattern that is visible from the top. We see the ugliness pulled through our lives' circumstances; we see the trials we have endured, but the breathtaking beauty of God's redemption tapestry is often invisible to us. Only when we understand that we are a part of the greater story are we changed.

I think of the biblical story of the refining of Sarah. She often doubted God and took things into her own hands to the great detriment of her marriage and family. Her deep anguish at not being able to have children was like a piercing cry before the Lord. Finally, she received Isaac, the child of the promise! Even though she couldn't comprehend the ultimate fulfillment of prophecy,

Sarah's joy must have been increased because she knew God had promised generations of blessings would come through her son. God was faithful to his promises, allowing Sarah to give birth to the many-timed great-grandfather of the Messiah. This very same Savior would come to save the whole world. Sarah was indelibly a part of God's greater story, though she saw very little of that story during her lifetime.

And what of Rahab? Outside of the family of Israel, yet faithful to a people and God she did not yet know. She protected the spies and God gave redemption for her and her family. Not only this, she was also named in the lineage of Jesus, after she married an Israelite, Salmon, and gave birth to the great-grandfather of King David. Rahab knew God was great, as she became a faithful follower of Yahweh even though she watched her city and culture destroyed by a conquering army.

Then, there is Ruth, a Moabite—outside of the family of Israel as well. She gave undying love to her mother-in-law and clung to faith when Naomi had lost hers. Boaz, her kinsmen redeemer, saved Ruth's and Naomi's very lives and fathered Ruth's son, Obed, the grandfather of King David. This same David, the beloved king of Israel who followed God with "all his heart" (1 Kings 14:8), would be the many-timed grandfather of Jesus, the Messiah. Ruth couldn't have known all that when she was a young widow who left her own family and culture to take care of Naomi. Yet she knew she was a part of God's story, and that was enough.

And, of course, there's Mary. An unwed virgin from a humble Jewish home, Mary's life was turned upside down when she was called to bring God's son into the world. Her fiancé nearly deserted her; her child was born in a stable far from her family and home; she was forced into exile for a time; and she eventually watched that son die on a cross. Even though she had a sense of God's greater plan, she must have had many questions about why things were happening as they did. She almost certainly had very little idea of the wonder her surrendered life had brought into the world—for all time and eternity.

Our greater story has been so changed by Mary's story of service to the Lord. Yet, the full beauty of her surrender will only be seen at the end of all things. On that day, we will see souls "from every nation, tribe, people and language," gather before the throne of God (Rev. 7:9).

Yes, there is a great surprise predicted in the heavenly vision when all the redeemed gather before God's throne one glorious day. There will be stunning beauty for you and me and all who accept the invitation to be a part of the greater story. So often we see only the pain and trial. However, we have the promise that we will gaze upon the grand fullness not only of our story, but also of the great story—as we live forever and fully within that one glorious never-ending day.

If we have committed our lives to Jesus, we are not our own. We have been bought with a price, and all we are is due to the great goodness of God. Nevertheless, we often sense that we deserve a good life. That God somehow owes us because he brought us into this world. But this is not the nature of things.

Although God does not owe us a good life, he longs to give us the best life. Too often we go through life with no understanding of what that best life is. But sometimes we catch glimpses of God's vision and of our place in his greater story. Even though the story is far beyond our human comprehension, God longs for us to see this "great beyond" of what he is doing.

I see glimpses of the greater story when my story touches the lives of others, especially those who feel adrift, bankrupt of God's goodness, who need to hear the testimony of my broken-yet-redeemed life. As you read my story, you can learn of God's great story. This is a part of why he has allowed all the hardships I have faced in my life: so that I may tell his story. I want you to know that beyond all the spectrum of human experience, there is yet a greater beholding, far beyond all we have known. And we will marvel throughout eternity at this perspective with its million layers of beauty.

Saint Mother Teresa of Calcutta said, "Pain and suffering have come into your life, but remember pain, sorrow, suffering are but the kiss of Jesus—signs that you have come so close to him that He can kiss you."[3] In this kiss of Jesus, we see that one kiss on that great and final day will be enough to melt away the horror of a thousand wars. All our pain and suffering will make us better able to see him. When all is made right and there is full redemption, the clearest, most radiant vision will be given to us.

Resting in His Perfect Plan

My loss of life as a mother was one of my greatest points of suffering. In the times when I was hospitalized, particularly in Hungary, I missed weeks of all the little moments of life with my kids. I didn't get to go to my daughter's costume party at school. I missed moments of two-year-old joy—coloring, singing, playing tag—with my son. I missed hand-in-hand walks with my oldest son as he returned from school. I will never get these moments back.

But are my losses the end of the story? If God is redeeming, buying back, all things, isn't there more to be told? Gloriously, beautifully, yes!

Romans 8:28 is often one of the most misquoted verses in the entire Bible. It reads, "And we know that for those who love God all things work together for good, for those who are called according to his purpose" (Rom. 8:28 ESV). Some read that as "Don't worry, be happy. It is all good." In one sense, that is the message of the verse. But it is absolutely not the primary meaning.

We have no guarantee that our sufferings will cease in this life. We can pray our hearts out, believe to the ends of the earth, and muster all our strength toward that end, only to be disappointed. At that point, we may say that the Bible is a farce and its promises are lies.

But our understanding of biblical truth is one-dimensional. We are looking at the linear nature of our lives and expecting good for these days alone. But with God, there is always more to be seen, heard, and known. He is the Alpha and Omega (Rev. 22:13) of all time, inhabiting eternity itself.

In *The Green Letters*, Miles J. Stanford says, "[God] is working from eternity for eternity."[4] Using an illustration from A. H. Strong, Stanford notes that when God wants to make an oak tree, he takes a hundred years, but when he wants to make a squash plant, he uses only six months.[5] The question, then, is "what do we want to become? An oak or a squash?" Most of us would choose to become "an oak," like the ones Isaiah calls "oaks of righteousness" made for "the display of [God's] splendor" (Isa. 61:3).

In 1 Corinthians 13:12 (ESV) Paul says: "For now we see in a mirror dimly, but then face-to-face. Now I know in part; then I shall know fully, even as I have been fully known." And as we look again at Romans 8:28, we need to remember it was written by Paul, the apostle who was shipwrecked three times, flogged, imprisoned, and most likely beheaded as a martyr. He goes on to reassure in Romans 8 that nothing can separate us from God's love. *The Message* conveys Romans 8:38–39 like this:

> I'm absolutely convinced that nothing—nothing living or dead, angelic or demonic, today or tomorrow, high or low, thinkable or unthinkable—absolutely *nothing* can get between us and God's love because of the way that Jesus our Master has embraced us.

This verse implies that some pretty hard things can come against us, but there is nothing, no nothing, that can separate us from the love of Christ.

As we look back on our journeys, we must lay hold of this redemption and rest in the plans of God. At times, we can feel like we are cut off from Christ's love. For those with mental illness, this often comes when our minds are compromised by the evil onslaught.

In my story, I glory that evil does not control my mind anymore. I am healed in many ways, treated, and fully in control of my mind. And I can rest in the assurances of Romans 8, that nothing can separate me—then, now, forever—from Christ's love. My own story of healing is one I give to you with the hope of sure redemption of your suffering too.

I have often dreamed of seeing the Northern Lights. I love the movement and surreal sheen in the pictures I have seen, but I am sure the pictures do not compare to seeing the lights in person and being able to add the third and fourth dimension of real life, the time and space of it. In part, I want to see this marvel because I feel it would bring me closer to heaven, to imagine the velvet contours of sky and land and sea. Yet, I know, even this glory will fall so very short of the grandeur of our future glory.

In Romans 8:18, Paul says, "I consider that our present sufferings are not worth comparing with the glory that will be revealed in us." *In us.* Not in the heavens or the earth or any other form of creation, but in *us,* the children of God.

In 2 Corinthians 3:18, Paul says, "We all, with unveiled face, beholding the glory of the Lord, are being transformed into the same image from one degree of glory to another. For this comes from the Lord who is the Spirit" (ESV). Our truest reflection is the vision of him, Jesus. One day we will see his glory fully, and then we will fully understand.

As I make my way home to the heights, home to God, like the character Much Afraid in *Hinds Feet on High Places,* I must hold the hands of other companions, including Sorrow and Suffering.[6] I will never forget the suffering I have endured. I do not wallow in that suffering, but I remember so that I will recognize how far God has brought me. I love the second verse of the hymn *Come Thou Fount of Every Blessing,* which says "here I raise my Ebenezer, hither by Thy help I'm come."[7] My life has become this continual raising of my *Ebenezer,* which in the Bible means, "Thus far the LORD has helped [me]" (1 Sam. 7:12). Sometimes it has been all I can do to raise, for the moment of a struggling breath, my hand in worship. But this is enough.

We are each on a journey of trust. As I move from suffering to redemption, trust has been essential. I trust in the goodness of God no matter what has happened to me. I continue to trust even though I have endured a very real hell of mental illness.

Nothing truly worthy in this life is easy. To experience redemption, we must go to the places of our pain and, in faith, grasp the unchanging hand of God upon our lives. We must rest in his greater plan, his goodness, his truth. I cannot see a way to view my journey with mental illness without this faith united with trust.

We are well on our way when we can say, "I know whom I have believed, and am convinced that he is able to guard what I have entrusted to him until that day" (2 Tim. 1:12). It takes more than steely resolve to make this statement, although some good ol' determination comes in handy. There also needs to be a softness that allows us to remain close to the love of God and the belief that what he has in store is far greater than what we have now. And we also need eyes set on eternity, even while we harness this glorious vision into the current moments of our lives.

Redemption nuances itself within us. We do allow ourselves to be purified, made new. We do surrender the whys. We do rest in the greater story. We do grasp God's perfect plan. But we also let redemption capture our here-and-now moments with love, joy, peace, and all the fruits of the kingdom. We dance when the music is heard, and we raise our gaze to a sky so glorious that our eyes take on a heavenly glow.

Redemption is real today. We can know, in a divine way, what is to come so that it changes what *is*. I speak into your life on this day, in this moment with this certainty. I speak humbly yet firmly, so that you can truly be free. Free to laugh. Free to dance. Free to sing. Free to behold all the realities of God in the great healing of your life yesterday, today, tomorrow, and always.

11

THE SUN IS RISING
From Closed to Open

June 2016

The air mattress that was our makeshift bed creaked under me, and I was instantly wide awake. I spent the first night in our newly purchased home in Orlando staring at the walls, fearing another round of insomnia, and wondering if I could fill this space with my presence since I felt so small and diminished.

As time grew short on our internship, which had included an apartment, we decided to stay in Orlando and, furthermore, to buy a home. God provided a beautiful house for us, but I remember little of the process. As we were closing on the house in May of 2016, I was spiraling out of control, soon to enter UBC. After my release on May 21, I was trying to comb through our possessions while again fighting for life and so weak, needing the help of others to make this move in mid-June.

My body was well enough after enduring two serious hospitalizations in less than two years, but my mind was still shaky. I had little self-confidence, and the shadows of dark doubts about God's power and ability to conquer evil were still haunting me. Depression's grip made each day a struggle, and I felt a mixture of self-loathing and utter lack of heart. It was difficult to see or believe that God had good plans for my life, and I was not sure I could win this continued battle for wholeness. I did not believe I would ever claim a future of victory and power and a sound mind. Although I wanted to believe that God desired good for me, I didn't know how to mentally focus on that grand future when I didn't know what I would face tomorrow—or even that night. How could I feel the security of the love of God when I didn't know what I could offer the world or my family?

When Everything Closes Up

Although it took time to realize, I now understand that I had closed myself off to God's plans and to the possibility of sharing my pain with others. I felt lost, utterly so. And God, who had long been my Abba Father, seemed so very far away. I was like a drooping flower bloom who could no longer open to the sun.

I could relate to the lament of Psalm 42:3–4 (ESV):

> My tears have been my food
>   day and night,
> while they say to me all the day long,
>   "Where is your God?"
> These things I remember,
>   as I pour out my soul:
> how I would go with the throng
>   and lead them in procession to the house of God
> with glad shouts and songs of praise,
>   a multitude keeping festival.

It had become difficult to shed actual tears because of the medicine I was taking, but my inner tears were many.

Abandoning my faith in God's triumphant plan for my life meant that I wrestled deeply to simply "do life." After Hungary, I had the cushion of a medical leave, a great and necessary gift. But after leaving the hospital in Orlando, I had a house to settle into, missionary support to raise, and kids to parent. I felt so defeated, especially when sleep didn't come easily.

I constantly wondered, "Will I ever feel good again?" This relentless perfectionism had claimed my life early and strong. My father would often speak this poem that he saw me living out, saying, "Good. Better. Best. Never let it rest till your good is better and your better is best." The continued drive for "best" would not give me a moment's peace, even when I saw no way of achieving it. I felt like I had been beaten up and down by the enemy. I was completely down for the count.

Another question also haunted me: "Will I ever be worthy again?" Worthy of friendship, motherhood, the status of a good wife. Terrible as all these struggles were—the deep depression, the waning of faith, the feelings of inadequacy—they were made much worse because I did not share them with others. I simply acted as though I had not experienced anything unusual. God was offering me the gift of vulnerability, which could liberate my life. But I left that gift unopened and tried to prove myself sufficient.

The sense of needing to prove myself had a vise grip on me. If I could just show everyone I was okay, then I would be okay. I wanted to put away everything that made me seem weak because then I wouldn't be weak. Or so I thought. As you can imagine, this didn't work out too well. It simply left me with a closed, charred soul, unable to open warmly and genuinely to relationship.

Faltering Feet

My therapist had encouraged me in the fall of 2015 to consider my bipolar diagnosis as a strength—a perspective I needed to hear. Yet, as I continued to work toward stability, I had to consistently assess my bipolar symptoms. I understood that this kind of self-awareness is important for anyone, but the constant inner examination made me feel more and more trapped. I couldn't get away from my pain and failure, but oh, how I wanted to do just that.

In those days, the freedom to be vulnerable became foreign to me. I felt like all the damning things were pointing toward me and my not-yet-truly-befriended bipolar disorder.

I want to be clear—this journey is nuanced and uneven. I had come to understand how my bipolar diagnosis could be a strength and internalized that I was "fearfully and wonderfully made" (Ps. 139:14). I had come to see that God could and would redeem every part of my life, especially my mental illness journey.

However, those little moments felt self-contained. I shifted from thoughts of hope and life to ones of anxiety and dread, from basking in healing warmth to shivering in the cold. I battled daily for the sunlight of embracing good things, but I felt weighted down by depression as I sought to regulate my moods and neurochemical balance. Sleep came intermittently; other nights I spent tossing, turning, and in anguish of soul.

I would like to act like everything was okay as soon as I remembered God's promises for my life and tie it all up with the bow of an apt lesson. I don't want to admit to the darkness I have known. However, I am describing the nitty-gritty of the journey I took to learn to live in the little moments with God and others. The struggle from bad ways of thinking to good ones has been just that—a struggle. Most of the time I have known that the good will win, that God will win. But not always.

The dark shadows of my second hospital stay nearly overtook me. I made it through only by enduring hideous, soul-freezing nights of insomnia one shaky breath at a time. As I look back, I can see clearly the pervasive, sovereign hand of God holding me—no matter how I felt. Through his mercy and grace I have lived to share my story.

However, the darkness is not forever gone. I still can feel shadows creep into my mind, and I dare not take off any piece of my spiritual covering. I know the truth and love of God in my heart, soul, mind, and strength, and I need it all in this journey.

And you do, too. Our battle, the one for our very lives, is not against our flesh and blood. It is against the powers of evil (Eph. 6:12). They march through our minds with their narratives of condemnation, doubt, fear. They are led by the thief who comes to "steal and kill and destroy" us (John 10:10).

I want you to hear me clearly. I am not saying that our battle is only spiritual and that our complicated brain chemistries do not need medicine. The scientific advancement of medical treatment to help stabilize those with mental illness is a blessing, and those treatments are essential for many in a difficult mental illness journey to make any progress. But I believe true healing involves much more. As a whole, this healing can result in a bright and pure openness to God and others. This openness in my life has brought me to this place and provided the strength and sense of self to write this book and share my story. We learn to trust God no matter what comes, our hearts receiving God's love and its accompanying strength. As this happens, it always translates to the desire to share with others how he has met us with his love.

The First Pink of Sunrise

Eventually it comes—that first softening pink of sunrise with all the promise imaginable for a new day. For me the first glimmers of sunrise came precisely on the heels of the dank darkness, and the colors of this new day brought a weightiness of promise. In Hungary, I caught a glance of the dawn when my beloved Jared read the promises of the Psalms to me in the hospital and when my twin sister, Sara, held my hand and promised me God would bring me through the darkness in decided victory.

I chose life when I looked into my two-year-old son's eyes as we played puzzles on the hardwood floor of our Budapest flat. I turned toward God's restoration when my darling five-year-old daughter hugged me with the joy of having a mother. Later, I saw God's provision when my seven-year-old son demonstrated resilience and happiness in a new life in America. These moments and so many others invited me to trust that there was a new day for me and those whom I love.

The sunrise of this new day deepened as I stayed the course in opening myself to God and others. Two months after my second hospital stay in Orlando, I wrote my first online post about my journey with bipolar disorder. I had previously shared the fragile, tender pieces with Keda, but I this was my first step in opening myself to the world.

I had been writing for years about my life, touching on matters like prayer, longing for home, the struggles of being a mom. Before my diagnosis, those things felt like less weighty topics. Yet, even then I had often felt afraid and intensely insecure to put anything I wrote out into the world. And now, it wasn't just anything. It was the ripped up and shredded fragments of my story, my life. The fear of giving away what I held so closely clung to me.

That fear can stop most of us, even when we trust that our story is good and our words worth sharing. It's hard, sometimes, to see how sharing our stories will open our hearts to the healing of God. But once we can begin to share, we recognize the truth of how we are most blessed, made whole through this offering of ourselves to others.

Maturity is required to bring our lives to God, offering ourselves to him. That's where we must begin. Our next step toward healing is improving how we interact with others. Paul says in Romans 12:1 that we are to offer our bodies as living sacrifices. I like how Eugene Peterson translates this verse in *The Message*: "Take your everyday, ordinary life—your sleeping, eating, going-to-work, and walking-around life—and place it before God as an offering." But the next decisive step is really seeing the people God has brought into our lives and deciding to live for their good. We have to empty ourselves, see their needs, and allow them to fill up what is lacking in us.

As we share our lives and stories with others, the very essence of our soul is strengthened. We find greater courage through the love of those we have touched. We are no longer hiding behind a tiny barrier of looking good before others. We are resting fully in God's love for us as we open to him and others.

This tiny barrier can manifest in many forms of perfectionism, but perfectionism does not allow us to truly display our best selves. Brené Brown writes,

> If we want freedom from perfectionism, we have to make the long journey from "What will people think?" to "I am enough." That journey begins with shame resilience, self-compassion, and owning our stories. To claim the

> truths about who we are, where we come from, what
> we believe, and the very imperfect nature of our lives,
> we have to be willing to give ourselves a break and
> appreciate the beauty of our cracks or imperfections.[1]

Appreciating this beauty of our imperfection allows us to be transparent with the full scope of who we are. A refreshing, even stunning openness captivates us and liberates us.

Perfectionism had long kept me wearing a mask or having one nearby to pop on when I felt like I wasn't enough. Then I came to a great paradox: *My bipolar episodes had fully displayed my human weakness, and now I could be grateful that these experiences had fully opened me up to God and others.* They revealed the glory of God's all-encompassing love peeking through my cracks and imperfections, and in this glory I could offer myself freely to others.

When the freedom of vulnerability becomes a way of life, we learn to be kind to ourselves. We receive the grace of our humanity, fully loved as we are, and we share this gift with others. As we look at the darkest moments of our lives, we find we can share them. We can raise up the hard things because in our great need, God has pursued us, found us, and loved us.

It is true that openness begets openness. When we don't hold back from discussing the hard elements of our lives, we invite others to do the same. This joyous community full of freedom is held tightly together in the love of Jesus.

He Knows the Plans

Even when we begin to open in vulnerability more and more fully, we will still face setbacks, which can be difficult to embrace as a part of God's plan. At one point, when things were otherwise going well, I experienced anxiety symptoms that contributed to tremors, which left me unable to drive. More recently, I began to gain weight, most likely due to one of my bipolar medications.

It's hard to deal with the fallout of mental illness, or chronic illness, or broken relationships. Heart-rending pain leaves us vulnerable to invasive doubts about whether God is truly good or whether he wants the best for us. We are left confronting this lack of trust in God.

While I say this humbly, I also speak it strongly: when you face setbacks in your journey, don't close up—either to God or others. This will only leave your heart sickly and shriveled. We all must fight this desire to retreat inward. We must continue to trust in the greater plan of God, readying ourselves for a sure and coming blooming of life.

We will always face an adversary who fights against our faith and our openness to God and others. Joni Eareckson Tada says, "Suffering is that last frontier [the Devil] exploits to smear God's trustworthiness."[2] We all are up against an ancient enemy, and we must see that we battle "the course of this world," the passions of our flesh, and "the prince of the power of the air" (Eph. 2:2 ESV) so we know how to fight.

The course of this world is so ready to denounce God for all the bad and bankrupt us spiritually. *The passions of our flesh* want things to be easy and instantly gratifying, and we rebel often when things are hard. And *the prince of the power of the air* wants to trap us in his destructive web of disbelief as he hates us and our faith. Ephesians 2 goes on to say, "But God, being rich in mercy, because of the great love with which he loved us, even when we were dead in our trespasses, made us alive together with Christ"

(Eph. 2:4–5 ESV). This life in Christ is quintessential to opening us to the new day.

I know I can't convince anyone of God's goodness. But perhaps my story can find some places into your heart. My pain, two times near death in the hospital, all my inner battles to stay well, and the fallout of my mental illness, have all been for good. I would not be the person I have become without these things. I have a well of compassion, depth of faith, and love for others who struggle in any way with life-altering hardship because I have been one of them.

But believing in God's goodness because of what has happened earlier in our lives is not enough. We must also be open to what is coming because the full purpose of our lives is pointing toward what is ahead. We can trust this good God is working in our lives. We can trust because his perfect power, will, and love are sculpting our lives as beautiful vessels. We are called to thankfulness for God's planting of us in this life. His desire is to grow us and cause us to bloom sweetly for his glory.

God's faithfulness extends to every possible perspective we can have for our lives. His truest plan is to draw us home to his embrace through everything, absolutely everything, that comes into our lives. It is all a gift. If the hardship before us draws us tighter into his embrace, then it is a part of his good plan, the best plan, for our lives. Even if we question and doubt, we will draw closer to God if we are true to the struggle and allow our wrestling to be a wrestling *with* God. We simply must continually remain open to him.

Henri Nouwen writes,

The more you are called to speak for God's love, the more you will need to deepen the knowledge of that

love in your own heart. The farther the outward
journey takes you, the deeper the inward journey must
be. Only when your roots are deep can your fruits
be abundant.[3]

Sometimes God uses difficult and painful experiences to help
us to grow. When my mother was in the last stages of her battle
with cancer, I wrote this piece that encapsulates what it means
to be on a true journey with God.

Funneled hope pours through the day's dismal tinge
And the spirit longs, yes, desires to live.
"Simply live," she says in a quiet, steady, ready voice.
Let me live the days given and find meaning true yet.
Let me take what it is to be and narrow and shape
Moments of action with the simple peace of life . . .
. . . for in the end, living is measured by its passion.
Not the flashing, daring kind, but the one
Which refuses to be anything but alive.
This is the life I choose.
No other is meant for me.

As openness to God continues, we see what he sees. Near the
end of my mother's life, God showed me the hallowed place of
unseen things, indestructible things. He also showed me his love
in an extraordinary way. The display of his intentional love left
me open, even in the greatest heartache I had yet experienced
in my life.

I drove home one morning and felt a sharp pain of emotion
as I prepared to care for my mother. It was difficult to breathe. A
hard ball burned in my throat, as my eyes pricked with tears. I

cried out to God, "God I can't do this. I don't have the strength to care for my mother, and wash her frail, cancer-ridden body!" Almost immediately, he directed me to 2 Corinthians 4:16–18:

Therefore we do not lose heart. Though outwardly we are wasting away, yet inwardly we are being renewed day by day. For our light and momentary troubles are achieving for us an eternal glory that far outweighs them all. So we fix our eyes not on what is seen, but on what is unseen, since what is seen is temporary, but what is unseen is eternal.

Then, I heard the Lord say to me, "I want you to look into her eyes. See how I am making her ready for her eternal home." And as I bathed her that morning, I looked into her beautiful blue eyes, and I saw heaven. I saw strength. I saw home.

In many ways, the road I walked with my mother's cancer prepared me for the road I walk with mental illness. I miss my mother dearly while navigating these destructive and uncharted waters. Yet, I know there are unseen things happening. With all the faith God has given me through Jesus, I believe something gorgeous is happening in me, which is for all eternity.

The purposes of God are full and rich. The harder the process, the more opportunities to cultivate deep change. This is the prize for not losing heart, not closing off to God and others. Yet, the truest prize arrives in the end when our arms opened *to* him will *get* him. We will rest fully and completely then in his embrace, his face-to-face love, and all the accompanying delights. Friend, open your heart, your life. You will receive far more than you ever imagined.

12

THE BRILLIANCE OF OVERCOMING
From Defeat to Triumph

June 2017

Early one morning, while Jared watched the kids, I ventured downstairs to the screened-in porch to engage in my daily quiet time with God. We had returned to Souderton, Pennsylvania, for the summer, staying at the mission house that had welcomed us many times before. I sat on a white, plastic patio chair, propped up my legs on another chair, and basked in the morning light that graced my face with a gentle warmth. I noted the canopy of the dogwood trees along the cemetery paths where I had shuffled a little more than two years earlier and was grateful for the progress I had made since we first returned from Hungary.

I opened my senses and my heart to God as I opened my Bible and journal. As I prepared to hear from God, I don't know what I expected to receive, but what happened next was nothing less than extraordinary. At first in small phrases, then in sentences and whole paragraphs, God spoke to me. The words I heard filled me with life. I had come through so much pain, and he knew what I had suffered. He knew the embarrassment and shame I carried. But he reassured me that my suffering was not the end. He told me I was beautiful in his eyes and that my life—even in these darkest days—was part of a great story to bring glory to him. He told me I didn't have to be afraid of what might come because I had faced the deepest darkness and watched him redeem it.

God spoke hope to me—an assurance of all the things I had once believed about heaven. He reminded me of the promise of Jesus's return to create a new heaven and a new earth. He spoke emphatically of the truth of his soul-deep healing in my life. He spoke and spoke and spoke until I could barely breathe for the joy of what he was singing over me!

From Death to Life

God spoke to me like I was altogether new in him. And I was. The woman who had twice entered mental wards in the past twenty-seven months had come through the fire and was refined. Those days of so much darkness and looming death were behind me. He was making a promise and urging me to hold it tight. I would not face the darkness I had once faced because he was bringing me from death to life in my mental illness journey.

It isn't easy to affirm with integrity the promise of not facing so great a darkness as I had in my major manic episodes because my struggle is chronic and ongoing. Mental illness, like any other physical frailty, takes us into heartbroken places where we grieve what has been lost. Although I still struggle with symptoms, the all-out war upon my mind is over. God has led me through the battle, and I can see the sun shining brightly. My faith gives me confidence that I won't be defeated.

Until that morning of sweet communion, doubt had haunted me. I feared that I might relapse or even be overcome by insanity. I could never seem to master the pull that the darkness had on me, and I feared that one day its lies would eventually take their toll and destroy me.

In my younger years, I always found it easy to rest in God's presence and could easily connect and hear from him. But it had become a constant struggle to hear from God after my manic episode in Hungary. My mind raced like ants from a destroyed anthill, scattering in a thousand directions. I was weary from my struggle for genuine repose of any kind, and I wondered what had happened to the woman who used to enjoy the peace and presence of God.

I had left my ministry job and moved to a job in sales, which fit me horribly and exacerbated the problem of my busy, disconnected mind. The same questions continued to bubble to the surface: "How long can I go on this way? Will I simply survive with my mental illness or will I thrive?" I longed for the latter but feared the former.

But on that warm June morning, every voice of death was silenced. God spoke overwhelming victory as the narrative of my life. He called me to believe it right then and there. My faith had been like a sputtering light bulb after my intense manic episodes and their accompanying lies, burning bright on some days while flickering dimly on others. But now! I embraced my hope, the surety of my faith, like the fullest sunshine of a cloudless midday sky. What has followed is a sweeter communion with God as the remembrance of that morning has continued to illumine my path toward the new day. God showered his truth on me, and now I know without the shadow of lingering doubt that nothing can separate me from his love.

My friend, God wants you to know this deeper life also. He desires to renew your life by speaking truth into you again and again. He longs to see you truly rise from death to life. Colossians 1 says, "He has rescued us from the dominion of darkness and brought us into the kingdom of the Son he loves, in whom we have redemption, the forgiveness of sins" (Col 1:13–14). God claims you as his very own for all time and eternity, and he desires that in this moment, as you're reading these words, his truth will set you free.

From Evil to Good

As I have written before, the Evil One wants nothing more than to destroy you. I believe mental illness is a part of our fallen, broken world but not spawned by evil. Therefore, mental illness itself is not evil. But the devil, the great liar, exploits our struggles with mental illness, making us more susceptible to patterns of lies, paranoia, and much more. He is the imposter, the thief, but not the true shepherd of our souls. He nearly destroyed my life, and he also wants to rip yours apart. His diabolical plans are bound in the lies he feeds us and his attempts to grow those lies. Yet, God is ever greater, infinitely rich in mercy, grace, and love.

It is easy to fall into a trap of shame and "less-than" thinking. Wanting to reach a "normal" place where I don't need medicine and treatment to maintain my mental wellness, I can hear whispers of lies telling me something is wrong with me and I am too broken to be fixed. Wanting to be free of those voices can make me want to skip treatment and venture out on my own. Doing so makes me more vulnerable to the lies and to the evil one who wants to destroy me.

Only recently have I been able to really think about my places of pain before, during, and after my hospitalizations. In those times, I felt like I was fully being handed over to evil. Yet, I have come to realize that even in those days, a sovereign God held me and everything around me in his hands. I don't write these words easily because the terror was so real. But when God poured into my heart that June morning, I recaptured my faith that he and his work are the greatest, most supreme, and sovereign of all.

In *The Great Divorce*, C. S. Lewis depicts a journey between heaven and hell. Those in hell are like ghosts, gray, ugly, and dead. Those in heaven are solid, grand, and full of color and life. Lewis depicts one man, a ghost living in hell, with a red, hideous lizard on his shoulder. This tiny, treacherous beast is incessantly lying to him. Yet, the man is terrified of the angel from heaven who is trying to remove it. During a struggle, the lizard warns that the man will die without him. Eventually, the man allows the angel to remove the lizard, and he almost instantly becomes a dazzling being, one of the "solid people" and the lizard becomes a great white stallion. The two become one and ride the heights of heaven with majesty and glory.[1]

Can It Be a Blessing?

And so we have come full circle to the pivotal conversation with my therapist that I described in the opening pages of this book. Can I truly view my bipolar disorder as a blessing, a strength? Will I really allow God to take mental illness and make it the source of great victory, a white stallion that I can ride to the very heights of heaven?

My mental illness has often felt like my red lizard—intertwined with me and speaking the most terrible things, calling them true. I have sometimes fought like the man in Lewis's novel against the transformation of my "lizard," my creature of lies, because I did not know who I would be without a mind full of all those limiting lies.

But given over to God, even this sickness of mind can become something beautiful and transformational. I am drawn into the love of God as my exposed mind sheds all the falseness. I am able to allow God to wrap me in his truth like a mother wraps her tiny baby in a soft blanket. As I grow in that truth, I am then able to crawl, walk, run, and ride the heights of God's fullness—his incomparable beauty.

What the enemy intends for evil, God is working for good. In all things, he is working good. There is not the picking and choosing as though he is somehow capricious. No, in and through every single thing, he is working good.

We see this truth when we think about the very real way God turned his back on his only begotten son. It was gut-wrenching for God the Father as his son cried, "My God, my God, why have you forsaken me?" (Matt. 27:46). He was on the cusp of death and descending into hell.

My father loved how the death and resurrection of Jesus is depicted in the old Carman song, "The Champion."[2] He decided it would be fitting for his memorial service because it meant so much to him. The song, a ballad really, sets up the crucifixion and resurrection like a boxing match. When the Son comes into the power, at least temporarily, of those who would defeat him, he drops his hands and becomes defenseless. Then, Satan delivers the knockout punch. It seems from all perspectives that Satan has won as Jesus is lying dead. The knockout countdown is being called, "ten, nine, eight . . ." But suddenly, life is stirring, and Satan is yelling because he knows he can't stop Jesus's victory.

This depiction is full of truth, and we trust in faith that the darkest moment of history, when God the Father turned his face away, is also the precise moment that bought our salvation, our redemption. Thus, every moment of our darkness, even when God seems far, will bring about our ultimate triumph. This finality of cosmic victory, as Jesus was victorious over hell through the cross, put the triumph of God in place over all time and eternity. This triumphant stance of God will never, ever, ever be shaken.

From Grave to Garden

As I look back, I realize that I did not just nearly die in the ICU in Hungary, I *did* die to all that I was before the manic episode. I had to rebuild my life from its most rudimentary foundation. My life's story was divided into "before the hospital" and "after the hospital."

However, as a believer in Jesus, I believe I was given new life when I first followed him, so this "death" in a hospital room in Budapest, Hungary, was one of plans, reputation, sense of self, and basic competency. "Buried" without a heartbeat of self-confidence, I remained physically alive, but barely. As I awoke in the ICU, my actual breath did feel like a hopeful victory. Then, I came to realize how much breath and hope and strength I would need to function as a wife, mother, missionary, and more. When I could not meet those needs, I felt like a lifeless form wandering in gray, barren places. In many senses, I *was* a ghost, ephemeral and insubstantial, longing for the life I had known but didn't know how to find again.

In the book of Romans, Paul says, "Who will deliver me from this body of death?" (Rom. 7:24 ESV). While I knew God could, I didn't know how to let him do that. I didn't know what it would look like to partner with him in that deliverance. I wished God would just change everything with one great miracle. He didn't work this way, although the breakthrough of that June morning reached deeply into my soul somewhat miraculously. But, the consistent journey, I gradually realized, was the path laid out before me, out of that grave, and it had to be walked step by step, breath by breath, moment by moment. It would not be easy.

I had to learn how to be in relationship with everything again. Even my life with my husband. I knew our medical leave after my Hungary hospitalization wouldn't last forever, and I also knew he couldn't sustain all he was doing to carry me and our three children, then ages seven, five, and two. It was hard, so hard, not to feel overwhelmed by the magnitude of the journey before me.

Yet I began to see, intellectually, that God did not want to bring me out of the grave just so I could dwell in some inhabitable land. No, he had prepared a pure and true garden for me. I continued to hear his voice of love and deliverance over me, and I clung to the promise that he would make my "wilderness like Eden," and my "desert like the garden of the LORD" (Isa. 51:3 ESV). My perspective became as clear as an azure sky, and the choice continually lay before me. I could see God as real, true to his word, faithful in promises, or I would have to view him as a charlatan, saying big things but unable to deliver.

When my choices were presented in these terms—golden and glorious or gray and gruesome—I knew which path I would choose. If I had survived the terror of those days in Hungary and

Orlando with even a "mustard seed" of faith, then I was confident that God could take that seed and move mountains (Matt. 17:20).

We each make the journey from grave to garden by continually acting upon our faith. We must trust that God's promises aren't too good to be true. We need to see with both a stunning clarity and radiant warmth that God is bringing about a new day.

But what does this process look like in our day-to-day life? As we faithfully walk toward wholeness, we learn that sometimes one breath of life, one slight glimmer of the coming sunrise is all we need to guide us. We come to understand that we must have patience with God's timing and patience with ourselves and with the process of healing. We have to stay in the process and allow him to uncover each place of beauty in our souls. We deepen our relationship with him as we learn his steps, his ways.

In my story, the process included finding God in the small steps, such as picking up my son from preschool. To drive the mile from my house to the preschool, I needed to make a harrowing left turn. Thinking about that turn would ratchet up my anxiety, making me tense, impatient, and fearful. Sometimes I would drive a much longer route to avoid that turn, but that detour left me feeling like a failure. To achieve a full victory, I had to go the hard way. Successfully swinging the car into the intersection made me proud. Seeing my sweet three-year-old and loading him into the van brought joy. I celebrated this simple victory because it helped me see how I could navigate toward the dawn breaking over a divinely prepared garden.

On another day, victory would look like having the kids' homework done and dinner started when my husband came home from work. When I managed to accomplish this feat, I felt "normal" in a splendid way and did some extra dancing, at least on the inside.

Sometimes, though, progress meant taking a midday nap and simply letting the love of God pour over me while I rested. Other times I demonstrated progress by hugging my children with arms strong enough to do so or letting my husband hold me because it had been a rough day or simply a rough moment.

Over time, we face thousands of choices that can lead toward health. Choosing to stop beating ourselves up over all we can't do. Choosing truth over lie, stopping the evil cycles of our minds. Choosing to engage in life and love and not retreat. We don't always make the best choice, but there is abundant grace when that happens. We learn above all things to put on love, which binds our lives together in perfect harmony (Col. 3:14 ESV). Most of all, we learn to never, ever, ever give up on God. His plans for us are good.

Gradually, the gray rubs off and the brilliant colors of the garden are revealed to our eyes. This garden comes to life by his Spirit that lives in us. Always in the garden, waiting for us, is our Savior, ready to commune. There is no sight of grave or desert, only a place filled with life. When we see the garden, we want to live here always. Sweetly, our Savior invites us to do just that.

From Defeat to Overcoming

That morning on the back porch of the Mission House stands as a place in time when God spoke his truth to me. I am an overcomer. He brought back to me a verse from Revelation: "And they have conquered him by the blood of the Lamb and by the word of their testimony, for they loved not their lives even unto death" (12:11 ESV). God declared that I had lived this verse through my near-death experiences and deep battle with mental illness. Its truth sealed itself as I began to open up my life and share my story with the world.

It has been a process of dying to write a book where my places of deepest pain are recorded for anyone to read. It is a death to myself and all the "better" things I would like to be known for—accomplishments that speak strength, success and competency. But I am now able to say that I wouldn't change my story for another one. In some ways, writing this book has been necessary for me to come to this truth and embrace every moment of my story. Yet, in other ways, fully embracing my story has enabled me to write this book.

God wants you to claim victory through your story. We can share the hard things because the love of God and his redemption are written over them. In other words, the process of overcoming continues as long as we refuse to forget what is true about our lives and ourselves as people. Though our hands may be trembling at times, we continually offer ourselves up to God and receive his courage to overcome. He never fails to grant us the victory.

So often, this process requires us to stand tall in who we are becoming, even if we only have a tiny particle of a vision of our overcoming selves. God is calling us to live as if this identity of strength is entirely true. As we see this bright, brave light shining through the darkness of our self-doubt, we focus our eyes on it. What we see is the strength, hope, beginning, home, intimacy, freedom, love, joy, peace, redemption, openness, and triumph for which we are created. With our tiny faith, we see pure light overcoming our dark sky.

I once thought the darkness was produced by mental illness. But I now realize mental illness is not what obscures the light.

Mental illness is how I have learned to come home to God, to his dazzling light, to all that his love promises. Mental illness is the conduit through which I have come to need and know God. God did not allow me to have a propensity for chemical imbalance to deliver me to evil. No. He allowed that feature so I would seek him, feel my way toward him, and find him, even though he has never been far from me (Acts 17:27).

The enemy thinks he successfully wields mental illness as a weapon to steal our lives, kill all goodness, and destroy every last layer of our identity. Many mistakenly agree, which leads to the shame and stigma that plague those with mental illness. But God speaks words of light, words of love, joy, peace, and all the fruits of the kingdom.

He says he created us in his image, beautiful and whole. And, if we let him love us in our struggle, this mental illness can become our greatest strength. The despair we feel from the battle can give birth to fresh hope. All the endings and grief of this painful journey can make room for unstoppable beginnings. The exiled life of our mental wilderness can draw us home to God. The loneliness of our isolation can propel us toward intimacy with God and others. The shame paved into this road of mental illness can usher in great freedom. The abject fear of possible outcomes can be transformed into love. The sorrow of our profound wounding can become a fountain of joy. The great war in which we fight for wholeness can lead to all-surpassing peace. The heavy hand of suffering can unleash the work of redemption. Our tightly closed tunnels of doubt can widen into a great openness to God and others. In all these things, what once seemed to defeat us can become our greatest triumph.

With every step forward, glimmering shades of glory are added to our vision. As the great hand of God stills our great upheaval, we glimpse the calming arrival of the first rose of sunrise, and we see the face of God more clearly as the sun rises higher into the sky. With this beholding, we realize that our million skies, our moment-to-moment perspective, will continue to reveal deeper, clearer, and more beautiful visions of him.

NOTES

Chapter One

[1] Dan B. Allender, *To Be Told: Know Your Story, Shape Your Future* (Colorado Springs: WaterBrook, 2009), 51.

[2] Timothy Keller, *Prayer: Experiencing Awe and Intimacy with God*, read by Sean Pratt (New York: Penguin Audio, 2014).

[3] Allender, *To Be Told*, 51.

Chapter Two

[1] *The Lord of the Rings: The Two Towers*, directed by Peter Jackson (2002; Burbank, CA: New Line Cinema).

[2] John Bunyan, "Giant Despair," in *The Pilgrim's Progress* (New York: P. F. Collier & Son, 1909), section 7, accessed February 4, 2021, http://www.covenantofgrace.com/pilgrims_progress_giant_despair.htm.

[3] Bunyan, "Giant Despair."

[4] Frederick Buechner, *A Room Called Remember* (New York: HarperCollins e-Books, 2007), loc. 204, 211 of 5189, Kindle edition.

Chapter Three

[1] *We Are Marshall*, directed by McG (2006; Burbank, CA: Warner Bros.).

[2] Henri J. M. Nouwen, *Turn My Mourning into Dancing: Finding Hope in Hard Times* (Nashville: Thomas Nelson, 2010), xv.

[3] Fyodor Dostoyevsky, *The Idiot*, trans. Eva Martin (Boston: digireads.com, 2018), 238 of 390, Kindle edition.

[4] Wikipedia, s.v. "Grandiose Delusions," last modified June 15, 2021, 18:47, https://en.wikipedia.org/wiki/Grandiose_delusions.

Chapter Four

[1]Eva Hoffman, *Lost in Translation: A Life in a New Language* (Lexington, MA: Plunkett Lake, 2011), loc. 2061 of 4838, Kindle edition.

[2]Timothy Keller, *The Prodigal God: Recovering the Heart of the Christian Faith* (New York: Viking, 2008), 103.

[3]Keller, *Prodigal God*, 97.

[4]Timothy Keller, "Not by Bread Alone," *Gospel in Life* podcast, Redeemer Presbyterian Church, June 17, 2007, podcast, 37:38, https://gospelinlife.com /downloads/not-by-bread-alone/.

Chapter Five

[1]Brené Brown, *Daring Greatly: How the Courage to Be Vulnerable Transforms the Way We Live, Love, Parent, and Lead* (New York: Avery, 2012), 12.

[2]Rend Collective, "My Lighthouse," MP3 audio, track 3 on *The Art of Celebration*, Integrity Music and Columbia Records, 2014.

Chapter Six

[1]Wikipedia, s.v. "Florida Mental Health Act," last modified January 7, 2021, 23:12, https://en.wikipedia.org/wiki/Florida_Mental_Health_Act.

[2]Bessel van der Kolk, *The Body Keeps the Score: Brain, Mind and Body in the Healing of Trauma* (New York: Penguin, 2014), 205.

[3]van der Kolk, *The Body Keeps the Score*, 205.

[4]van der Kolk, *The Body Keeps the Score*, 235.

[5]"Mental Health Disorder Statistics," Wellness and Prevention, Johns Hopkins Medicine, accessed February 13, 2021, https://www.hopkinsmedicine .org/health/wellness-and-prevention/mental-health-disorder-statistics.

[6]Alice Louise Kassens, Jamila Taylor, and William M. Rodgers III, "Mental Health Crisis During the Covid-19 Pandemic" The Century Foundation, accessed June 16, 2021, https://tcf.org/content/report/mental-health-crisis -covid-19–pandemic.

[7]Tanya J. Peterson, "What Causes Mental Illness? Genetics, Environment, Risk Factors," HealthyPlace, updated October 23, 2019, https://www .healthyplace.com/other-info/mental-illness-overview/what-causes-mental -illness-genetics-environment-risk-factors.

[8]Brown, *Daring Greatly*, 61.

[9]Brown, *Daring Greatly*, 11.

[10] A. W. Tozer, *The Pursuit of God* (Camp Hill, PA: Christian Publications, 1993), 81.

[11] Benj Pasek and Justin Paul, "This Is Me," performed by Keala Settle, MP3 audio, track 7 on *The Greatest Showman: Original Motion Picture Soundtrack*, Atlantic, 2017.

[12] *The Greatest Showman*, directed by Michael Gracey (2017; Los Angeles: 20th Century Fox, 2018), DVD.

[13] I Am They, "Scars," MP3 audio, track 4 on *Trial & Triumph*, Essential Records, 2018.

Chapter Seven

[1] Jonas Myrin, Matt Redman, Chris Tomlin, and Tim Wanstall, "Endless Hallelujah," MP3 audio, track 11 on *10,000 Reasons*, Sparrow Records, 2011.

[2] Henri J. M. Nouwen, *Seeds of Hope*, 2nd ed. (New York: Image Books, 1997), 170.

Chapter Eight

[1] Ann Voskamp, *One Thousand Gifts: A Dare to Live Fully Right Where You Are* (Grand Rapids: Zondervan, 2011), 49–50.

[2] B. Ligertwood, "New Wine," MP3 audio, track 11 on *There Is More*, Hillsong Music, 2018.

[3] C. S. Lewis, *The Lion, the Witch and the Wardrobe* (New York: Harper-Collins, 1950), 169.

Chapter Nine

[1] Heather Holleman, *Guarded by Christ: Knowing the God Who Rescues and Keeps Us* (Wheaton, IL: Moody, 2016), loc. 32 of 192, Kindle edition.

[2] Wikipedia, s.v. "Persecution of Christians in the Roman Empire," last modified February 9, 2021, 21:14, https://en.wikipedia.org/wiki/Persecution_of_Christians_in_the_Roman_Empire.

Chapter Ten

[1] Brian Doerksen, "Refiner's Fire," compact disc, Vineyard Music, 1990.

[2] Wikipedia, s.v. "Lament," last modified February 5, 2021, 20:08, https://en.wikipedia.org/wiki/Lament.

[3] Mother Teresa, *Love, a Fruit Always in Season: Daily Meditations from the Words of Mother Teresa of Calcutta*, ed. Dorothy S. Hunt (San Francisco: Ignatius Press, 1987), 91.

[4] Miles J. Stanford, *The Green Letters: Principles of Spiritual Growth* (Grand Rapids: Zondervan, 1975).

[5] Stanford, *The Green Letters*.

[6] Hannah Hurnard, *Hinds Feet on High Places* (Wheaton, IL: Living Books, Tyndale House, 1975).

[7] Robert Robinson, "Come Thou Fount of Every Blessing," 1758, verse 2.

Chapter Eleven

[1] Brown, *Daring Greatly*, 131.

[2] Joni Eareckson Tada, *A Place of Healing: Wrestling with the Mysteries of Suffering, Pain, and God's Sovereignty* (Colorado Springs: David C. Cook, 2010).

[3] Henri J. M. Nouwen, *The Inner Voice of Love: A Journey through Anguish to Freedom* (New York: Image Books, 2010), 94, Kindle edition.

Chapter Twelve

[1] C. S. Lewis, *The Great Divorce* (London: Geoffrey Bles, 1945), 98–103.

[2] Carman, "The Champion," track 9 on *The Champion*, A&M Records, 1985.

ACKNOWLEDGMENTS

It's with a good amount of fear and trepidation that I write my thank yous to memorialize in this book, which has been years in the making. The truth is that I will miss very important people because so many have been there for me in this book and life journey. So, if you are one of those dear people, please know your support has meant the world to me.

To the God of glory, thank you for redeeming my life, satisfying me with good, and healing me from the darkness! You are the light in every sky, the beauty of the stars and sun, and all the shades of their rising and setting. And because of Jesus, you are my sky, my eternal vision, and I will forever behold you!

To my Jared, a dedication and acknowledgment are not nearly enough. I rejoice that we have known healing together and will join, one day, in the Great Dance of a Forever Healing.

To JJ, Susie, and Samuel, thank you dear children of my heart for giving me more grace and love than I could imagine. Thank you for making me feel like a rock star for writing a book and for understanding when it took me away from you! I love you to the farthest galaxy and back!

To my dear (identical) twin, Sara, so many times you talked me through new words of criticism about my work in this book. You did what you have always done, going before me to protect me (except when we were born). You have made me laugh when I could have cried because it all felt so hard. Thank you.

To Kristen, thank you for loving me enough to come and be with me during those dark days in Budapest. You truly see me, and I love our friendship. Your presence in my life brings a great sense of wholeness.

To Linea, thank you for "fighting the good fight" in all you have endured. Your prayers throughout this journey, both with mental illness and this book, have been invaluable.

To Jonathan, thank you for being so passionate about this story of overcoming. You always remind me what it looks like to fight for life no matter what comes our way.

To Jennifer, my sister at heart, thank you for your depth of kindness and loving so well as we cared for Dad. Your support meant so much as I finished my edits while Dad was in his last days.

To Dad and Marie, thank you for your prayers over the years for this book. It was my great wish that you could read my book together, but God had other plans. Thank you, Marie, for loving me and us all these years.

To Mom and Dad Alleman, thank you for coming to Budapest in those hard days, especially you, Mom, with all the plane rides you have done for us! Thank you for seeking to understand something as hard to understand as mental illness and for loving me as I am. You both mean very, very much to me.

To Maribel y Jason, gracias siempre para tus oraciones y siempre creyendo en lo que Nuestro Señor puede hacer con nuestras vidas. ¡Les quiero!

To Aunt Debbie, you have loved us all so well since Mom went to Heaven. Thank you for seeing me as a writer when I didn't see myself that way and for *all* you have given.

To all my peer reviewers who cared enough to take the early manuscript and enter it whole-heartedly: Tery-Ann, Carrie, Tamara, Debi, Angela, and Danelle, especially, because of your intentional prayers.

To my small group in Florida, thank you *all* for the love and prayers and walking *with* me in this journey.

To April, thank you, for you have been a true friend on this long road home.

To Dave and Keda, thank you for offering your home and your hearts to help me complete my manuscript, giving support and community all the while.

To Kelley, thank you for praying me through and pouring hope again and again into this book!

To Dave and Courtnee, thanks for giving me the freedom and encouragement to write this book!

To Priscilla, thank you for so much laughter and many good runs together as I was healing.

To Wendy, thank you for your cheerleading spirit and unending encouragement in this journey.

To Amy, you were absolutely top-notch, and this book would not be here without all your help.

To Michelle D., your selflessness in coming alongside me and your beautiful endorsement of a rough manuscript mean the world to me, just like our friendship.

To Michelle B., your support has meant the world to me, and your kind correction has been priceless! Thank you!

To Dr. Daniel, thank you for being so wise and pivotal in my journey.

To Dr. B., thank you for walking with me in the tough places and keeping me laughing through it all.

To Judy, thank you for being more than a mentor, but like another mother in the absence of my own.

To Gina, thank you for your open-handedness in making connections for me and answering rookie questions.

To my agent, Don, thanks for taking a chance on me and giving so much for little in return.

And finally, Jason, thank you for believing in this book and an unknown author and coming to the rescue of my manuscript! Thank you, Tammy, for your thorough work in the editing process and making this a book ready to be born. And finally, Mary, thank you for taking all those last-minute hitches in stride and being so accessible. And to everyone affiliated with Leafwood Publishers, thank you!

DISCUSSION
QUESTIONS

CHAPTER 1

Mental Illness Doesn't Write My Story

1. Do you allow anything other than God and his redemption to write your story? If so, what? And why have you let this happen?

2. Like Abigail's therapist, has anyone said something pivotal to you that changed the way you thought, for good or for bad? If so, what did they say? How did it affect you?

3. What would it look like if your greatest weakness became your greatest strength?

CHAPTER 2

Learning How to See

1. What has been your most hope-filled moment? Did it come
   at a happy or hard time? Why did it give you hope?

2. Have you ever felt alone in your hope? As Abigail shared
   her understanding of hope, what did it make you think or
   rethink about how you experience hope?

3. Is it surprising to you that Abigail would experience hope
   while her husband read from Psalms, and she rested? Why
   or why not?

CHAPTER 3

The Openness of the Morning

1. Have you ever thought of grief as something that results from anything other than someone's death? What other kinds of grief have you experienced?

2. When you think about it, have you given yourself the space to grieve your endings? Why or why not?

3. Share one beginning that came on the heels of a significant ending in your life, like a marriage after a heartbreak, or a new experience after a special one ended.

CHAPTER 4

Warm Hues Beckon

1. Have you ever considered yourself an exile or in the middle of a wilderness? Why or why not?

2. How does Abigail's imagery of eating dust and drinking from dry rivers strike you? What have you sought in your life more than the eternal, life-giving waters of God?

3. What does the word *home* mean to you? What do you most look forward to in the Homecoming of Heaven?

CHAPTER 5

The Colors of Your Mind

1. Have you ever been hurt by someone you considered a good friend? Getting only as specific as you want, share how that hurt affected you and your trust in others, or even in God.

2. Can you identify with Abigail's sense of isolation? Why or why not?

3. Do you think Abigail is right in saying we cannot be fully sustained on God's love alone in this life because we need the community of others, too? How are you doing in the tension of both a healthy relationship with God and with others?

CHAPTER 6

Brighter Days Coming

1. Have you ever felt ashamed of something about yourself?
   How have you been working through that shame?

2. Why do you think the church can be such a shameful place
   for those with mental illness or other struggles? How can
   you make this situation better?

3. Abigail shares her rally cry of "No More!" when it comes to
   shame. Why must we speak so strongly to something like
   shame? What happens when we say "No More!" to any feeling or thought *not* from God?

CHAPTER 7

Crimson Covers the Darkness

1. What have you been most afraid of in your life? Has that fear ever come true? If it did, how did you deal with it?

2. Why is the context of a verse like 1 John 4:18 so important? What happens when we see that "perfect love casts out fear" in the longer passage of 1 John 4:14–18? How can this make us look differently at single verses of Scripture?

3. Have you found a quiet space or experience where you can easily feel God's love? If so, what is it? If not, how can you find a way to connect deeply with God's love?

CHAPTER 8

Dancing at Sunrise

1. What has been the most sorrowful experience or season of your life? Why was it so hard? Did you find joy after this?

2. Did you ever feel like your world was shattered into a million pieces? How did you recover, or have you recovered?

3. How can you intentionally implement Abigail's process to reignite, rewire, and refill your thought life? How does this connect so strongly to experiencing joy?

CHAPTER 9

The Beauty of Stillness

1. What experiences in your life have most disturbed your peace? Because we have all experienced the Covid-19 pandemic, in what ways has this crisis robbed you of peace?

2. Does God truly want us to know peace? If so, why does he allow us to live in a world that brings so much war instead of peace?

3. Abigail says, "God is our peace." What does that statement mean to you?

CHAPTER 10

All Turns Golden

1. Is there any real answer to the suffering of this life? Be honest in your response.

2. Abigail talks about "Surrendering the Whys" as the only real path through suffering. What are some "Whys" you might need to surrender to God?

3. Abigail shares about the song "Refiner's Fire" that she used to sing. Is it your heart's one desire to be holy and set apart for God? If yes, how does that change your view of suffering? If no, what is holding you back from the desire to be refined by God?

CHAPTER 11

The Sun Is Rising

1. What is the posture of your life right now? Are you more closed or open to others? To God? Why is this true?

2. Abigail believes strongly that being vulnerable with others in sharing our stories, our lives, brings healing. Do you agree with this? Why or why not?

3. What is one thing you can do today to open your heart more to God and/or a good friend? How might this change your perspective on life?

CHAPTER 12

The Brilliance of Overcoming

1. Have you, like Abigail, ever had an experience with God that was a breakthrough in your understanding of life? What was it? Do you think of it as a moment in time, or does it still affect your thinking and feeling?

2. Is there any "little red lizard" in your life—a thing you are unwilling to surrender to God because you think you need it? What do you think would happen if you truly gave this issue—whether a secret sin, place of shame, or other nagging thing—to God?

3. After having journeyed with Abigail through her story, do you believe she truly has moved from defeat to triumph? Do you believe God wants to do the same in your life? Why or why not?